MW00514163

HELL NO!

Raymond D. White

Cold Tree Press
Nashville, Tennessee

Published by Cold Tree Press
Nashville, Tennessee
www.coldtreepress.com

Printed in the United States of America
ISBN 1-58385-113-5

(LACK OF) DEDICATION

Have you been waiting with baited breath to have a book about hell dedicated to you? I'm not surprised to know that you haven't, because no one I have talked to is waiting for one to be dedicated to him or her either. Given the response I have received, I have decided that no dedication is a safe dedication.

Hell NO!

Contents

PREFACE

L et me begin by saying that the concept of hell is a pernicious idea that has infected much of Christianity and much of the rest of the world for too long and for no good. The idea of hell has made people miserable, separated people from each other, and given people a reason to maim and kill other people. We have never needed hell and we now need to banish it—maybe we should just send it to hell.

A definition:
Hellion (hel'yen) *n. Informal.* Someone whose theology is not complete unless a lot of other people wind up in Hell. [Probably altered from dialectical *hallion*, scurvy person.]

…well, this is not exactly the way the dictionary had it, but it pretty much tells the tale on hellions.

A recent poll revealed that sixty-nine percent of those questioned believed in hell. Given the ubiquity of Hellions, that is no surprise. Hellions seem to be everywhere…singing praise songs in close harmony…praying with the President…cluttering the TV channels as they raise money to keep YOU, MY FRIEND! out of Hell…beaming that same message out over the radio waves…

telling the State Department what to do about Israel…retrofitting churches all over the place with roll-down screens and power point capability…showing how great our country is by exercising their God-given first amendment right to call the founder of another large-cap faith a "demon-possessed pedophile" …praising each other for exercising their God-given first amendment right to call the leader of another large-cap faith a "demon-possessed pedophile" …preying with the President…putting notes into boxes of cookies to alert you that you are going to Hell if you aren't one of them…putting messages on the signs in front of their churches to alert you that you are going to Hell if you aren't one of them… exhorting on the street corners to let you know that you are going to Hell if you aren't one of them…blowing you up if you aren't one of them…making a list and checking it twice…

All of the world's large-cap exclusivist religions appear to generate a significant percentage of devoted Hellions among their adherents, and the Hellions appear to be the loudest talkers in each bunch, so it's hard to get away from them. Anyone looking for the easy way to start a successful religion (non-profit or otherwise) can take a lesson from the Hellions: if you want to get big you need to have an out-group, and you need to make sure "your" group gets told over and over again that they are "in". "It is going to be us on the inside at God's right hand and them on the outside burning in Hell." It has worked time and time again.

Too many people are worried about Hell—some of them have been worried literally to insanity about it. More than too many TV channels are cluttered with televangelists selling fire insurance. Too many people are wasting their time worrying about how to stay out of Hell when they should be worrying about how to live the life God has given them. Too many people are shooting or blowing up other people because the other group hasn't bought what "we" are selling and is going to Hell. For a heavenly host of reasons Hell needs to be dispatched.

I've had it up to here with Hell; I got worn out with Hell and hellions long before the current crop of hellions learned how to tie their own shoes, let alone took to the airwaves. But the hell of it is the Hell problem appears to be getting worse instead of better. It just doesn't seem to want to go away on its own, so we are going to give it a good shove—and have some fun in the process. It is time to get rid of Hell and hellions both. Together, in the pages that follow we are going to put salt on Hell's tail by using the hellions' own rules to evaluate whether as human beings we need Hell, whether Hell makes sense, whether Hell is fair to all concerned, and whether at the end of the day the God of love is going to be proud of Hell. We are going to do a job on Hell.

Reader discretion is warmly advised. If you feel that you might be offended by this book, the ideas expressed herein, the publisher, the author, the printer, the guy who drove the truck to bring it, the bookseller, any of their family members, or their advertising agency, stop reading now, convene a warm and caring family group and burn this book in the comfort and sanctity of your own lovely home. Purchase a second copy and send it to a friend who can burn it in the same type of loving ceremony in the bosom of his or her own family. Get a third copy to put in your files; you will have to start another fire sometime and it will be good kindling.

In spite of deciding that a dedication of this book would be a dangerous act, I do wish to thank in particular some of those whose help and encouragement were an important part of bringing this volume from wild idea to reality. The hard working few include my wife, The Reverend Linda White, for putting up with this project, The Reverend Professor David G. Buttrick for his help and encouragement, the Reverend Daniel Patrick Mcgeachy for his early encouragement, the late Martin S. Roberts, Jr., P.E., for asking the question that put the Third Half into proper focus, and William Snyder, for his help and encouragement. There are others, too…

Concern with Hell is particularly prevalent in the Bible belt where I grew up, so I got a good dose of Hell early on. From the get-go I was not happy with Hell as it was being presented. One kept being told that one might end up in Hell, and that was worrisome, but the more I thought about it, the more I was irritated by the fact that the whole deal didn't seem fair to a lot of people. In addition, some aspects of the Hell that was being touted didn't seem to make sense.

Hell NO! is a statement of the new Christian paradigm. It is an in-your-face approach to theology that concentrates on demolishing Christian theology's remarkably central dependence on Hell, a dependence that has not just Christians, but people of all kinds of exclusivist faiths looking down upon, hating, and literally killing people who aren't members of their faith.

I confess that as serious as the problem of Hell may be, there are so many idiotic aspects of the formulation of Hell that I can't help laughing at it. *Hell NO!* is—or at least it tries to be—a book of serious theology, but because when you really think about it, Hell is so damned funny, and because straight theology can be as hard to take as horehound drops, *Hell NO!* softens the blow by using humor, sarcasm, exaggeration, sneak attacks, jeering, heckling, and logic. In other words, *Hell NO!* embodies all of the aspects of church politics that you have come to know and love. There are kinder, gentler, and far more scholarly books out there that are saying the same thing. Two that I warmly recommend are *If Grace is True* by Phillip Gulley and James Mulholland and *The Heart of Christianity* by Marcus J. Borg. They will do you good. *Hell NO!* may also do you some good; at the very least it will deal with hell much more ruthlessly and efficiently than the recommended companion volumes, and it will be a lot more fun.

This volume is divided into three halves (Reaganomics lives in our hearts if not in our minds). In the first half the approach will be to use hellion reasoning to examine the need for Hell from the human viewpoint: What actions or failures to act will get us into Hell? Is Hell really necessary? Were we to have to do without Hell, would its loss be a major disappointment to the people who were sure they weren't going there anyhow? Since this is an Interactive Book, you will have the opportunity in the first half to pencil in the names of some special people whom you think have earned a berth in Hell and who didn't come up on my radar screen.

The first half will convince you that Hell has to exist. To convince you we will:

- Examine the rules under which one can obtain a berth in Hell. Unfortunately, we will not be able to discuss and enjoy each of the possible sins, and there will be no explanatory photographs or explicit drawings. A lot will be left to the imagination, but, in spite of the lack of illustrations, you are going to get a basic working knowledge of how to go to Hell—or, by reversing the socks and wearing them inside-out, how to avoid Hell.
- Pay a well-deserved tribute to Dante Alighieri, a justly famed pioneer in the field of hellology.
- List from life experience some of the folks who most obviously deserve to go to Hell. We will describe some

of the problems they have caused, but truth to tell, this being but a slim volume, we will only make a brave beginning at a definitive list. You will be able to add to it from your own experience.

By the time you are adding names to the list of the Hell-bound, you will be well convinced of the need for—nay the absolute inevitability of—Hell. You will have found enjoyment and fulfillment in ferreting out the guilty and in being a part of making sure they are punished according to their crimes. You will have the warm feeling that comes from knowing your tithe dollars that pay the operating expenses for Hell are truly doing the Lord's work. Unfortunately, just when you were ready to relax after a job well done, we will go on to the second half.

The second half of the book will consist of an examination of Hell from the point of view of God. What place does Hell have in God's scheme of things? What good is it going to do? At the end of the day is the God of love really going to be proud of Hell? (By the way, what is God like in the first place?) This second half, like the first, will be based on strict application of good engineering principals. Brick will follow brick into the wall of logic that will either fence us into Hell or out of it. At the beginning of the second half there will be a road map of what is to come. No point in going into detail here—you'd probably be like me and forget. At the conclusion of the second half we are going to come to the shocking (for some) conclusion that Hell does not exist.

In the third half we will try to sort out the irritating mess that has been made by the first two halves having led us to opposite conclusions. We will look at some of the ramifications of our Final Conclusion—the one that says that Hell doesn't exist. Some readers will not be happy. We will be left to wonder whether theologians like the beloved C. S. Lewis, who otherwise had a lot of good ideas but just couldn't bring themselves to give up Hell, and who bent over backward in high heels to justify the actual need for Hell, will be really hacked off as we decide that in the end Hell does not exist. If they are hacked off, we could just suggest that they go to Hell and leave us alone, but we will take a kinder, gentler course and suggest that they get comfortable with the idea of meeting even people like us in Heaven.

HELL NO!

Raymond D. White

INTRODUCTION

Creation's Groaning

In his letter to the Christians at Rome, Paul wrote "the whole creation has been groaning in travail together until now…" Did Paul's remarkable prescience bring to his ears the sounds of the tectonic plates, far below the earth's surface and unknown to others, as they groaned against each other? Had he experienced an earthquake, or had he heard the rumblings of a volcano? Perhaps all those things were true, but they were not the whole story, for he went on to say "and not only the creation, but we ourselves, who have the first fruits of the Spirit, groan inwardly…"

Paul may indeed have understood that the earth is a living organism, changing and moving, actually groaning as it wrenches itself from one state of existence to another, but he knew too much about people to believe that nature was the only cause of the groaning of the creation. He knew that his brothers and sisters in Christ, as well as the very creation itself, groaned under the weight of human failure, hubris, hate, fear, laziness and a thousand other follies.

Nothing has changed since Paul wrote those words. The tectonic plates—known to us now—still grind against each other,

1

earthquakes and volcanoes still shatter the quiet and snatch lives away, and people are still people—even when they have heard the "good news" of Christ. Our follies are without number. Perhaps the love of money is the root of our follies; perhaps it is the quest for power, perhaps it is a flight from fear. Whatever demons drive us, they continue to drive us from one folly to another and another and another, with no end in sight.

One of the follies that keeps those who have the first fruits of the spirit groaning is the idea that Hell is waiting and that "we" know the way to avoid it. For centuries, many Christians have embraced this folly, as have many of the followers of other religions. The idea that "we," and only "we," have the key that unlocks the door that allows escape from Hell has convinced too many people that they are special, that they are superior, that everyone else should believe exactly what they believe, and that those who do not believe are at best inferior and suspect, and at worst are useless, valueless, and even subjects for extermination.

The idea of Hell has been too much with us for too long, and it has done the world nothing but hurt. The state of the world today suggests that the very idea of Hell and "our" knowledge of how to escape Hell are too often being used to separate "us" from "them", and this separation is the cause of at least as much of the world's evil as is the love of money. It may well be that the fear of Hell and the pride of having dodged that bullet may actually be in the lead when it comes to causing evil.

It is time for us to take a hard look at Hell, call it the impostor it is, and get it behind us, so we can concentrate on living like children of the God of Love and stop living the lives of people who are scared of going to Hell, or of people who think we have some special relationship with God because we have said the magic words and are saved from Hell—unlike the unwashed billions who haven't said the magic words. We need to concentrate on bringing ourselves together by the mysterious, incredible, unfathomable love of God rather than on separating ourselves one from another based on someone's idea of who is going to Hell.

Forty-odd years ago, as a young Navy officer, I made my first trip to Europe and Britain. I saw many things I have not forgotten but one of the most memorable of those new things I saw in the old world is not just a memory, it now seems to be a portent of the future—our future in the new world. What I saw was churches, from huge cathedrals to tiny village chapels, that were empty. Their congregations were either completely gone or were reduced to tiny remnants that were struggling more to keep the building intact than to come closer to God.

Coming from a city that has often been described as "the buckle on the Bible belt", I was used to seeing churches everywhere, and I was used to seeing them vibrant and full of people. As I looked at the empty churches of the Old World, I was both astonished at their emptiness in the midst of crowds of people and certain that such a thing could never happen in my country.

The churches of the Bible belt and its buckle still seem to be comfortably full, but I fear that in too many cases they are full for the wrong reason. Too many people are in church because church is the place to get saved from Hell and to find out how to succeed (read "make more money") in this life—all too frequently at the expense of those disposable, unsaved people who aren't in "our" church. This approach to religion is the one that is used in a broad variety of Christian denominations and in other religions as well, but it is an approach to God that takes us, instead, to Hell—in more ways than one. It is, in my opinion, also an approach that will ultimately empty most of the churches of the new world as it has already done in the old world.

This book is an attempt to help get rid of Hell and focus on the God of Love. This is a time to put our fears behind us and embrace ideas that might be new and that will work better than some of the old ideas. I hope you will meet some familiar ideas as you read, and perhaps you will even meet some new ones. Hopefully you will be able to join me in laughing at Hell and getting rid of it at the same time.

Many devout Christians resist any thought of change in their faith, believing that any new ideas have to be wrong, and fearing that the Faith cannot stand the change of even the smallest of its supporting doctrines lest the whole structure collapse completely. This approach to Christianity is an approach that gives a centrality to Hell, and an emphasis on avoiding Hell that overpowers almost every other aspect of the faith. Combined with avoiding Hell is the assurance that having adopted the magic formula that keeps one out of Hell, one has also achieved a favored position with God that will bring with it riches and success in this world.

These folks' idea of who God and Jesus are (is?) is, unwittingly for the most part, founded on the idea that Christianity has no underlying reality, but is wholly a construct of the dogma that we have received, and that without the totality of the dogma there is no reality in Christianity. Taken to the extreme, this approach holds that there really is no God and that the only thing that exists is our idea of God, and that somehow the idea of God is more potent than the reality of God.

Other Christians find in the blossoming of a new Christian paradigm an affirmation of their faith, a faith that that has changed and grown stronger as the years have passed, but that has been at odds with the tradition with which we have lived. To those of us who feel that way, the new paradigm comes not only as an affirmation; it comes as a source of hope for the future of Christianity.

For many, this welcoming—not without some fear—of the new Christian paradigm is a source of relief because we no longer have to engage in Coleridge's "willing suspension of disbelief". Parts of the faith that have been unbelievable no longer have to be believed. Ideas about God that once reeked of logic and common sense, but couldn't be accepted because they were outside the circle of commonly accepted truth, now can be accepted, lived by, enjoyed, and shared as part of the revelation of a God who really does love us—and treats us in the everyday world in which we live, and in the hereafter, as if we really are loved.

Those who can neither believe in nor accept any change in their faith can rest in that faith, but those of us who have been having trouble making all the pieces of the faith fit together are released by the new paradigm to create a new mosaic of faith that can change our lives because we can believe that our faith is truth.

The Origin of Hell (The Quick Version)

The truth, in spite of what a lot of well-meaning people may think, is that Presbyterians did not invent Hell. Saint Augustan (5th century CE) was a warm supporter of Hell who contended in *The City of God* that "the fire and the worm" of hell eternally torture the dammed and that the ability of human bodies to withstand the punishment of Hell forever is "a miracle of the most omnipotent Creator." To say that this is impressive thinking is putting it mildly, and to say that this is an impressive miracle is putting it even more mildly. Augustan was clearly working overtime and had been drinking too much coffee when he came up with and explained that one.

The early Christians (along with various other small cap religions that were starting up at the time) were able to use the musings of still earlier civilizations and religions in addition to their own deepest longings as they fabricated the definitive version of Hell that we now enjoy. The Egyptians got into it fairly early, and were among the first, if not THE first to incorporate into their world view the idea that what happened to you after death had a moral component: you slept eternally in the bed you had made during life.

The Gilgamesh Epic, of Babylonia in the early third millennium BCE, was an heroic (in more ways than one) attempt to deal with what happens after death. The key players in the Epic were Gilgamesh himself, Enkidu, Uruk (a place), Utnapishtim, Enlil, Ea, and a serpent. Between them, they pretty much concluded that the land of the dead is an unpleasant place, and that once you have gotten there you really don't have a serious chance of getting back. Not exactly a nice picture, but it wasn't full-blown Hell.

The Jews were not as concerned with the possibility of Hell as we have become, thus they did not spend any significant amount of time worrying about what Hell might be like or what you had to do to stay out of it.

Using these and other early attempts plus their own vivid imaginings, and a variety of ideas that the Greeks and Romans had been passing around for years, Christians seem to have been extremely important players in the formulation of our world's view of the possibilities opened by death. Like most of the other players, the Christians eschewed simple rotting after death. Again like most of the other players of their era, they came out strongly in favor of Hell. Unlike most of the other players, however, they also included Heaven and a way to get there. Heaven was not a totally novel idea, but it was an idea that was warmly received by a world that up to that time had had only a modest amount of encouragement about the chance of there being a heaven and the chance that one actually might end up there. But, Heaven or not, Hell was in the middle of everything, big time. And here we are, with too many of us still dealing with Hell, modern age, enlightenment, modern ideas, digital computers and all, not withstanding.

Hellion Theology

A casual look at the American scene—and I suspect that this holds just as true in any other scene where you can find "religious" people—makes it abundantly clear that for an awful lot of people, theology just isn't theology unless there are a goodly number of other people who end up in Hell because they didn't do/say/believe/practice what you do/say/believe/practice about God and humankind. In the theology of these good people there has to be suffering, and it is always on the part of someone else—at least they are pretty sure it will be someone else.

This approach will be referred to as Hellion theology. One of the most powerful tenets of Hellion theology is the idea that a wrathful God is waiting for you at the Pearly Gates, and that if you aren't one of the elect, you aren't going to skate past Him: you are going to fry. This belief on the Hellions' part is not mere supposition on my part: there has been more than one actual sighting of "A Wrathful God is Waiting for You" on a sign in front of a church. [Note to alert reader: This is not made up; I have seen one of these signs, in rural Smith County, Tennessee.] At the heart of Hellion theology is the fact that at The Gates themselves you will not have a chance to fake it. There will be no gun-decking. You may have pulled the wool over a lot of eyes during your sinful years on earth, but this is the BIG one and you aren't going to fool God. Unless you have been washed in the Blood of the Lamb, you are going DOWN.

So, according to Hellion theology, if you aren't one of us, the washed, you might as well get ready to burn. Justice and righteousness are going to prevail and a sorry, unsaved dog like you is going to be found unjust, unrighteous, and wanting at that big weighing-in in the sky. There is an abundant supply of Hellion theology out there—at least along the roads I travel. You don't have to wonder about it: there are plenty of GET RIGHT WITH GOD signs to make the message clear.

The Hellion theology crew are the people who have the

IN CASE OF RAPTURE
THIS CAR WILL BE UNMANNED

bumper stickers. There is a very high probability that you, having read this far, are one of the unwashed, one of the people who has an

IN CASE OF RAPTURE
PLEASE LEAVE THE KEYS IN YOUR CAR I NEED IT

bumper sticker. According to the true Hellions you are going to fry forever; and they have their key rings attached to their belts with long chains: you are not going to get their cars, either.

There is a surprisingly large number of people who believe fervently in Hell for others, and sport hopeful bumper stickers about going to Heaven themselves, but who, believers or not, according to the REAL Hellions are going to wind up in Hell because these would-be Christians aren't Hellion (orthodox) enough in their belief. The Hellions will gladly tell you that there are going to be a lot of surprised people at the gates of Heaven— many of them ordained elders and pastors of well-known denominations whose names begin with Presbyterian and Episcopalian, as well as others. If you are a serious enough Hellion, all you have to do to find some of the Hell-bound is look around you: probably two or three of the people in the same pew with you are going to Hell.

Our study of Hell is limited to approaching Hell from only two directions: from the point of view of humankind and from the point of view of God. (In other words, we aren't going to be looking at Hell from the point of view of dachshunds, fox terriers, or other appealing quadrupeds, although they will be mentioned from time to time.)

Let us now consider God, but keep in mind that we will do so from the Hellion point of view. Moving quickly through the key points of Hellion theology: God is powerful. God is just. God created everything. God is in complete charge of everything. Everything is part of God's plan. God has weighed us and found us wanting—thus deserving of a permanent berth in Hell—but, being a neat guy, God has allowed at least a lucky few of us to skate around this problem by providing a way for us to get saved. Our job is to get saved, which is quite simple if we are fortunate enough to get the Word and react appropriately. Tough luck if you happen to have been born into a Zoroastrian home in the fastness of the Tora Bora mountains where neither the U.S. Marines, nor the missionaries have been able to penetrate!

From the Hellion point of view, the whole salvation thing is pretty straightforward. We Hellions are right proud of Our God, because Our God can beat up your second-rate, geeky God. Our God is a powerful God, and we have plenty of hymns and have

9

preached plenty of sermons to keep us reassured of just that fact. We are going to make sure that you know that the power is on our side: bigger, tougher, more just, more powerful, able to leap anything in a single bound, that's our God. We feed on the power of God, but our God of Power exacts a toll: you go to Hell if you aren't on the right side of Him. We Hellions, however, are on the right side of Him. Too bad about the rest of you.

Even as I write and as you read, there are well-paid construction crews working on a large flameproof expansion of Hell. "Why all this construction?" you are no doubt asking. The reason is simple. There are just a helluva lot of people who need to go there. Be honest. You run into them every day, don't you? You are not one of them, of course, and not me, either, but what about him, the guy with the beer gut and the four-wheel drive pickup? The one who never uses his turn indicators? The one who throws his empty beer bottles in the ditch in front of your house? You have the picture. So, if they are all supposed to be there, there's gotta be a Hell, right?

Using Hellion rules, Hell is necessary, and if it didn't exist we righteous Hellions would be downright burned about the omission. Life would be flat and stale if we thought everybody else was going to get away with stuff on an eternal scale, particularly if we have been good and they haven't, but even more particularly if we have gone to the trouble to get saved and they haven't. After all, like the famous Captain Leathers said when he heard about the Steamboat Inspection Board, "What's the use of being a steamboat captain if you can't tell everybody to go to hell?" Hell is no mere luxury, no figment of an overactive imagination: it is a Hellion necessity.

Having Hell available for sinners is a part of the sense of justice shared by Hellions and non-Hellions as well, but we have to remember that justice is not the only card in the game: we are also dealing with the love of God. But love or not, your Hellions are not going to be happy without Hell, and they aren't going to give in without a fight. So let's join 'em, let's think like Hellions, let's use Hellion rules, and let's send some people to Hell. Forever.

Entropy, the beloved Second Law of thermodynamics, may not seem to have much to do with God, human nature, or Hell— but it does. The lighter of dictionaries don't mention entropy (statistically there isn't much call for the word when compared to the calls for words like 'parse' or 'depilatory'). The heavy model dictionaries, however, embrace it fully. For our purposes, the thermodynamic definition of entropy is the operative one: Entropy is the measure of the amount of energy in a system that is not available for doing work, that is to say, entropy is the measure of how random, disordered and useless the system has become. Thus, the higher the entropy, the more the confusion and the less the potential for good.

The Second Law tells us that entropy is always increasing, or put another way, that the entire universe is unraveling. Presumably, when it all started, the universe was in a highly, perhaps perfectly, ordered state, but ever since, second by second, it has been becoming less and less organized, more and more ragged. The Second Law tells us that, in the words of J. R. Newman, "entropy is the general trend of the universe toward death and disorder." Every careful observation and experiment that has been carried out to test the theory, or law, of entropy has shown that all systems are, indeed, drifting toward a state of inert chaos. [Note to alert reader who didn't take Thermo: No kidding here, entropy is really true.]

If you have passed the age of 45 or 50, you are all too aware that this drift is happening to your very own body and mind, and that your friends of a similar age are similarly afflicted. Unless you are still in the face-lift mode, you have also recognized that nothing is going to stop the deterioration.

Just as this law of thermodynamics holds true for all the other systems, it seems to be equally true for the moral system. I am reminded of the Methodists. Their methodical approach to God led them to conclude, *inter alia*, that we need to be saved from the clutches of sin, so they have directed a lot of effort toward getting us saved and keeping us that way. It was hard enough to get people saved in the first place, but alas, the observations the Methodist leadership made of those who had been saved brought to their attention the fact the not everyone seemed to *stay* firmly saved. Some dropped back into their old ways of lying, thieving, boozing, harping, griping, and other indications of a lack of salvation. What to do?

First the Methodists named it: Backsliding. Then, whether they realized what they were doing or not, the Methodists began grappling with the problem of moral entropy. True, the folks in question had been saved from sin, but some were unable to resist the continuing tug of sin and slid backward into its grasp. There was still hope for them, of course. Prayer, admonition, and example, sometimes coupled with stouter forms of encouragement, might bring them back into the ranks of the saved, and, if they happened to shuffle off this mortal coil while they were back in the fold, they were good for eternity in Heaven. However, if death called while they were backslid, they were doomed. Hence it was important not to be found by death, or let others be found by death, in a backslid condition.

This possibility of Damnation-without-warning that the Methodists were grappling with seems logical from a Hellion point of view, but it does seem rather mean spirited on God's part to send someone Down forever just because they happened to die on the one day they were backslid, even though they had been saved continuously for years before, and probably would have gotten back out of trouble during the next week or so if only they had had the time.

Unless you are one of those cave-dwelling holdouts who is still trying to resist Original Sin, you can consider the backsliding situation to be a manifestation of Original Sin, or to put it another way, if you don't think you are a sinner, you can consider backsliding to be a manifestation of moral entropy. It is easy to conclude that we don't have to fight to be bad, but we usually have to struggle to be good. It seems that we are naturally hell-bent, and that moral entropy, just like regular store-bought entropy, is always increasing.

You have figured out by now that backsliding into the inert chaos of sin and dissipation is the moral field's equivalent of the Second Law's inevitable growth of entropy, and your own observation of everyday life has probably convinced you that we humans seem to work overtime trying to thwart the best efforts of Methodists, Baptists, Presbyterians, and a host of others to keep us out of Hell. So maybe the Hellions have a point: unless they save us from it, we are Hell-bound. Let's consider what Hell from the Hellion point of view might be like.

In the unlikely event you haven't already made up your mind on this, you will soon realize that looking at Hell using Hellion rules and the nature of humankind as our starting points inexorably draws us to the conclusion that Hell does exist. In fact, we are quickly going to reach the conclusion that it has to exist. Let's enjoy.

THE FIRST HALF

*An Examination of Hell
from the Hellion Point of View*

BIBLE STUDY TIME

We can't ask any honest Hellion to give up on Hell without a fight, so let's do a little Bible study to see if there is any support for a Loving God who wants to meet most of us in Hell.

On the Hellion side, we can read that you can be condemned:

He who believes and is baptized will be saved; but he who does not believe will be condemned.—Mark 16:16

(It doesn't quite say what the victim has been condemned to—could be a lifetime of listening to bad rock music instead of bad praise songs—but it does say condemned, and that gives a Hellion hope).

We can read that you might end up in Hell:

If your eye causes you to sin, pluck it out; it is better for you to enter the kingdom of God with one eye than with two eyes to be thrown into hell (on earth, maybe?)—Mark 9:47

And there is a ton of ink spilt on judgement in both New Testament and Hebrew Scriptures, but, in fact, most of the judgement scriptures are warnings not to judge or are discussions about people judging each other (for good or ill), and most of those references don't quite say what the result of the judgement is going to be. Still, you can get the feeling that you might end up in Hell; here's an example:

> *For if we sin deliberately after receiving the knowledge of the truth, there no longer remains a sacrifice for sins, but a fearful prospect of judgement, and a fury of fire which will consume the adversaries.—Hebrews 10:27*

There it is, and if you want to believe it, you can. (If you are going to believe this one, however, you had better get ready for trouble because you must have heard the truth, and I know you have dome some deliberate sinning since then—haven't you?)

> *For any one who eats and drinks without discerning the body eats and drinks judgment upon himself.—I Corinthians 11:29*

Can this really mean that you go to hell forever for eating a pork bar-b-que sandwich? Maybe judgment isn't really that final—or maybe God is a really mean dude?

> *The rich man also died and was buried; and in Hades, being in torment, he lifted up his eyes, and saw Abraham far off and Lazarus in his bosom...—Luke 16:23*

If you had enough cash to actually buy this book, it looks like you are in trouble. There are poor people lying at the door all over the world—people who will never in their lives have enough disposable cash to purchase a book like this—and you are not one of them. Lucky for you if you are so poor you had to borrow this book.

… Then death and Hades were thrown into the lake of fire. This is the second death, the lake of fire; and if any one's name was not found written in the book of life, he was thrown into the lake of fire.—Revelation 20:15

This looks serious. You had better bust your can to make sure you are written into that book. Too bad, of course, for those who never knew there was a book, or couldn't get to the scribe so they could be written in. But that's just life with the God of the Hellions in charge.

And you, Capernaum, will you be exalted to heaven? You shall be brought down to Hades. For if the mighty works done in you had been done in Sodom, it would have remained until this day. But I tell you that it shall be more tolerable on the Day of Judgment for the land of Sodom than for you.—Matthew 11:23, 24

The folks in Capernaum had a chance and muffed it, and even though this is about eternity, you don't get a second chance from the God of the Hellions. Jesus is reported to have said the above right before he said "I am gentle and lowly in heart… my yoke is easy, and my burden is light." This is a confusing juxtaposition to a simple lay person, but, then, confusion is par for the course in Hellion theology.

We could go on with this, but you get the idea: there is ample scripture that discusses hell, or hades, or the lake of fire, or whatever you cotton to. There may be some question as to whether all of these references really are to an eternal situation or whether they may be referring to something more human scale and temporary, and for our sake, the more question the better.

The Topography of Hell

Since we are about to send a bunch of people to Hell, it might be fun to think about what today's what's-happenin'-now Hell is like. Nearly seven hundred years ago in Tuscany the brilliant Dante Alighieri (1265-1321) in his Divine Comedy (first published under another name) had an insight into Hell that rings true today. The truth is, no one has done Hell so well since, and this book is not an attempt to best Dante. Dante gave us a timeless vision of Hell, but what he really gave us was a vision of life. In chronicling the wretched inmates of Hell, Dante was giving us a catalog of how not to live. We were being told how to live if living wrong was the ticket to Hell; he hoped we would get the message and choose to live right. As this book unfolds the case will be made that how we live our lives will have nothing to do with whether we end up in Hell, but that how we live will be a measure of how much we love God.

In presenting this offering, I'm not trying to suggest that Dante missed the mark at all, or that this book is in any way up to the standard he set, however there are some important things that separate us from Dante's time and his writing, and they need to be honored. For instance, since it is not a widespread problem, we don't worry too much these days about simony (the buying and selling of church offices), but in Dante's time it was big enough and bad enough to get you down into level eight of a nine level Hell. (Don't think they aren't doing a little simony now, they are. But now that we have Enron, WorldCom, and all the ".coms", simony is a much smaller part of immoral and illegal global commerce and we just don't seem to care about it.)

In addition to changes for the better (if you can call ".coms" better), there have also been changes for the worse. In that respect, we would note that Dante never had the chance to have his day brightened by all the clever variants of voice mail, so he wasn't able to deal with all of the opportunities we face. (More about voice mail, later.) I flatter myself with the belief that if Dante had the opportunity to encounter them he would loathe the more vile aspects of voice mail, and that on that basis alone he would approve of the present undertaking. That may seem to be a major stretch, but Dante was deeply interested in the subject of Hell, and it would seem to follow that he would be interested in serious, scholarly updates of his work. Hence this effort, offered without shame or apology. (Okay, I am ashamed and I do apologize.)

There is some support for the idea that Dante's original name was Durante. The thought arises that he may have been encouraged to change it by his relatives who did not want to be associated with an author whose main claim to fame was a book about Hell. (Of course, Dante also wrote about Heaven, but who remembers?) In any event, we must give Dante the highest possible praise, not only for his courage and his wonderful insight into the hereafter—and the present—but also for the fact that he was able to express it brilliantly in the difficult medium of terza rima—fortunately for those of us who write about Hell these days, a now-defunct mode of expression.

Dante divided Hell into nine levels with the Executive Level being the lowest, hottest and smelliest. (Actually, in Dante's Hell the people in the Executive Level were frozen in ice, but that just doesn't seem to jar the modern sensibilities quite enough, so we are going to go along with all of those

Devil-with-a-pitchfork pictures and use at least a smattering of heat for our executive level.) Dante also had a neutral area for people who did neither good nor evil during life. This type of performance is considered so unlikely in the real life of today that there is no neutral area in "our" Hell. We do, however, give a Merit Award for people who did their best to go to Hell but for some unfortunate reason were unable to qualify. We will just leave purgatory out of this discussion.

In addition to creation of the Merit Award and dropping the neutral area and purgatory, Dante's Hell has been simplified by reducing the number of levels to four. Perhaps in the current throwaway, industrial age we are simply not as inventive in sinning as they were in Dante's time when everything, including sin, was hand made. On the other hand, maybe we don't have the fine appreciation for degrees of sin that the average man of seven hundred years ago seemed to exude with every word and breath. There wasn't that much else to do back then, particularly for the people who had time to write a book: if you didn't have crops to tend or wool to card, you either had to sin or contemplate the folly of those who did. A reduction to four levels seems to create a system that is adequately descriptive of the horrors to be required in a modern day Hell. It also seems to allow an adequate division of sinners into the levels of torture they so richly deserve, so it works for us.

Our Hell is a serious place, and you don't get there just by fooling around. There are carefully thought out and strictly applied rules that govern who goes and where they end up. After all, Hell is forever, and you wouldn't want to be stuck there on the basis of a casual decision or a bureaucratic snafu. Forms are all filled out in triplicate and are reviewed and re-reviewed by trained workers. There are no misteaks; sending people to Hell is handled just as successfully as the Texas court system handles handing out death penalties. For those strict legalists among you, the rules for going to Hell are presented in the Appendix. Let's move on to a brief description of who is in the four levels of Hell.

The levels have not been conceived in a frivolous or careless way: they exist because they have to exist. There are people who are clamoring to get there, and it would be positively unkind to deny them the fate they have worked for so hard and that they so very richly deserve. We are simply being there for them. They need us, and as devoted Hellions, we need them. It's not exactly " Killing a Kommie for Khrist", but you could call it "Jamming a Jerk for Jesus". I hate myself when I do this, but just keep on doing it. Omigosh! Is this an 0-3, or a 1-1, or maybe a 2-9??? (See Appendix.)

Consider yourself a great gal or guy; you are doing your part and you are all heart.

So Just Who in Hell is in Hell ?

With all the appealing possibilities available for eternal torture, you know there have to be some really nifty people who need to be tortured. Otherwise, why bother with Hell? It is, after all, expensive to run a really good inferno. In fact, since the life of the facility is infinite, the life cycle cost is also infinite. If you are an economy-minded Devil, you don't want to spend that kind of money without a real reason. The following lists are not exhaustive. You, of course, will know of quite a few special people who deserve The Trip. A blank page has been thoughtfully added at the end of each level to give you room to add important names and categories.

As you consider who to send to Hell:
- Do remember that Hell is forever.
- Don't make light judgments.
- Don't make snap judgments.
- Do your victim a favor and sleep on it.
- Make the first entry in pencil and then go over it with ink later when you really are sure.

Merit Awards

- Men who comb hair over their (very large) bald spots. Guys, it just doesn't work! Since you don't seem to be able to get this idea through your heads, we'll give you some time to think about it. Come to think of it, you are going to have eternity to think about it. That's just the way it is down here. But don't come completely unglued—you'll get to spend eternity with all the women who keep wearing "sweet, gay and girlish" outfits and/or miniskirts long after they should have stopped. They, of course, will be in line just behind the women who use toothpicks in public. (For some reason, men can use toothpicks anywhere and it is perfectly all right. I have never understood why men can use toothpicks anywhere, but they can. Maybe men are just hopeless.)

  Perhaps it has something to do with the fact that badly faded tattoos look worse on women than they do on men, and toothpicks are naturally associated with faded tattoos. (You can see that I'm trying hard to figure this out, but I just can't.) Well, fair or not, that's just the way things are down here—on earth, that is. 0-1 NOTE: These little numbers are the number(s) of the rule(s) under which the client qualified for Hell, or at least for a lousy merit award.

• Speaking of tattoos, women who have industrial sized leg tattoos get a merit award. 0-1, 0-5. If they have defaced a particularly well turned leg they get Level Two. 2-4.

• People who can't think of anything to put on their vanity plates other than a rehash of the kind of car they are driving: "MY240Z" etc. This would be a level two offense except for the sadness we feel upon contemplating a life that is so empty. 0-2

• Third face lift on the same face. 0-3

• People who think the government knows everything. Of course the government people who told them that are in level Two. 0-5

• Wearers of ankle bracelets. 0-1

• The waitresses (somehow they always do seem to be female) who work in the type of restaurant that I frequent, that is to say, the cheap type of restaurant where they have some kind of plastic cover or stained wood table top and no table cloth.

  The smiling waitress zips up to your table and plunks down the silver—make that "the eating tools"—right on the beautiful table top. This is really snappy, but the thought that always goes through my mind is, "You have a Hell of a lot more faith in the cleanliness of this table top than I have." I know what I dropped on the table last time, and I'm afraid to even guess what someone else has slopped onto it. Even more frighteningly, I have more than once watched the same waitress "clean" ten tabletops, chair seats, catsup bottles, and other assorted items using the same dirty rag dipped in the same dirtier and dirtier water. The whole thing reeks of Hepatitis B. But I'm a sport. I just wipe the utensils on my tie—gets the celery bits and dried gravy off along with the germs—and go right ahead and eat. These girls have probably poisoned more people than the Borgias, but they do it with a smile. 0-5

(Of course, this could become a 4-9, and that would have rather more serious consequences for the perp.)

Raymond D. White

THIS PAGE FOR LISTING OTHER MERIT AWARD WINNERS

Level One

THE INNOCENTS (Well, they really aren't that innocent)

The qualificants (I love this word) for Level One (Irritatingly serious) are those who...

- 1-1 cause a lot of minor irritation
- 1-2 do a bunch of hating
- 1-3 aggravate the Hell out of people
- 1-4 smile excessively
- 1-5 do excessive fake laughing

Level one is home to a lot of people you either know or see every day, or at least much too frequently. They are the ones who tend to irritate that tar out of you and who, more often than any other single group, cause you to thank God there is a Hell. Level one is also home to those unfortunate innocents who listened to someone else's bad idea and then went out and put it into practice. Many of these people were actually under orders, and for them we have to have a special level of pity. Unwitting Nazi concentration camp guards fall into this category, and contemporary American hotel maids are in mortal danger of Level One. Others, of course, weren't under anyone else's orders, but did it all on purpose and, usually, with malice aforethought. For them we have no sympathy, and if they were really good at what they were doing, we do have a lower, hotter level. Level One does have a lot of people who had the right ideas about how to get deeper into Hell, but just plain weren't good enough to get there.

- Gum poppers. Actually, gum poppers are *ON WARNING STATUS*. As you might guess, this means they can be sent to Level One if they do it just ONE more time. Reminds me of that wonderful sign seen in almost every real engineering office: "Tired of what you are doing? Want new thrills? Like to meet new friends? Want to see new places? Well, just screw up ONE more time!!!" Let's face it: no one pops his or her gum just once. 1-1

- Messing with someone else's Windows Icons. 1-1

- Sports announcers who talk about "ath-uh-leets". On a bad day, this can be extended to "Sports announcers who talk." 1-1

- Whoever invented the half page for ads that hangs out from the Sunday comics is going to be right here in One. I have, however, found out that you can tear the thing off without looking at the ad. In fact I did it this morning and wrote the note about this entry right on it! 1-1

- People who get their pictures in the newspaper more than once a month for being at society functions. This is dangerous to your health: excessive repetition can result in orders to a lower level. 1-1

- The first newspaper problem: We refer to puns and double entendres in newspaper headlines. The stories themselves don't seem to suffer over much from this problem, so we have to blame it on the headline writers. They are doomed. However, I am authorized to give everyone a break: there's an amnesty for all past sins. If you never do it again, you are saved. Ha, ha, ha...Like there's a chance in Hell that they will never do it again!

This sin falls into two categories, the general news and the sports news. One feels that it is most egregious in the general news since some of those stories have content of reasonably lasting importance. Hence, those headline writers may actually be in line for Level Three. On the other hand, it is just worse, worse, worse in the sports news. Hence those headline writers may actually be in line for Level Three. 0-1, 0-2, 0-3, 1-1 [Stuff*] OOPS! According to the rules, these guys are actually in Level Two!

* See the Appendix for a definition of Stuff.

The following examples were taken from only some of the papers in one tiny part of the country. Multiply this by an entire nation of readers and cry.

"STATE'S NEW PLATE DAWNING IN 2000"—the new Tennessee auto license plate had a rising sun on it (Funny, that rising sun was on the governor's campaign stickers last year. Some people think it looks more like a fried egg on green toast. They are right.)

"AN INVASION OF ART"—the art exhibit has paintings from Normandy, from whence they sent out William the Conqueror, and to whence we sent the D-Day fleet. What this has to do with art is anybody's guess.

"DENTIST GOES EXTRA MILE FOR SMILE"—No comment.

"MAGGIE WINTERS: A MATTER OF FAITH"—the actress in the new TV series is named Faith Xxxx.

"CAR SALESMAN WANTS TUNEUP FOR JOB'S IMAGE"— probably a forlorn hope, no matter what the headline.

NOTE: The next news writer or radio or TV newscaster who refers to snow as "the white stuff" is doomed. Level Two at least. Of course all of those who follow the next one go to Hell, too. In addition to the regular pleasures of Hell, they'll have to read or listen to their own stuff forever.

"VANDY SWAMPED"—the game was played in Florida against the Gators (who live in swamps.) Get it?

"...YELLOW JACKETS READY TO STING NEXT OPPO-NENTS"—Oh, well, Georgia Tech strikes again.

"FHS FIELD HOUSE BACK TO BLOCKS"—could this have something to do with concrete blocks and construction?—must be something about a track meet. Maybe they are starting over. Have you ever seen a field house running? There just wasn't any way to figure this one out without reading the article—some people just know how to torture, don't they?

"NFL LIKELY NOT PRICELESS MUCH LONGER"—Peerless Price is probably going to sign to play in the NFL.

Speaking of sports, let's talk about the Olympics. You might be thinking, "Oh, golly, the Olympics are being kicked by everybody in town. Does he have to dump on them, too?" Be relaxed. Nothing gauche is about to happen. It is true that everybody with access to a barrel of ink has smeared the International Olympic Committee, particularly the subcommittee tasked with looking the other way when the bribes are flaunted, but I am not going to touch a hair on their heads. Nor am I going to point the finger at the fine members of the medical staff who make sure the drugs are all administered by board certified physicians. Nope. The ones who have earned Level One (because of serious trashiness) are the crew who decides what constitutes an Olympic sport. They were doomed the minute they let beach volleyball in the door. 0-1, 0-2, 0-3, 0-5 [Stuff] *WHOOPS!* These suckers ended up in One in spite of a friendly effort to judge them at the Merit Award level.

COMMENTARY ON ABOVE: I have a bad feeling in my stomach when I contemplate beach volleyball as an Olympic sport. I mean, phuleeeze! And if that isn't enough, I fully expect to see skate boarding next time out. (By the time you finally get around to reading this it will already have happened.) It's just too much for an old time purist who still thinks that if we want a good Olympic team we should just go out and buy ours like every one else buys theirs. Of course, now we can.

Speaking of getting theirs, if the beach volleyballers have theirs, I want my favorite sport in the next Olympics: *HIGH SPEED LANE SHIFTING. HSLS* has been taking place for as long as there have been interstate highways and vast urban streets, yet it has never received the official recognition it deserves. Just as seamen have died traversing narrow straits in order to preserve the freedom of the seas, people have given their lives to keep the dream of HSLS a reality. They must not be forgotten. We must make their memory live with an Olympic moment.

- Excessive humming. (It doesn't take much of this to create excess.) 1-1, 1-3

- Radio/TV announcers who always manage to make it sound like something really, really big has happened on the stock market: "The market SANK OVER three points today!" "Stocks ROCKETED MORE THAN five points today in heavy trading!" "New York stocks PLUNGE OVER four points today!" 1-1

- Radio and TV announcers who make everything sound breathlessly important. C'mon, give us a break. 1-1

- Anyone who has ever done the voice-over for a movie trailer; they make everything, no matter how boringly trivial, seem unbelievably important. 1-1 (I think there actually is only one guy with that low, gravely voice who does them all. The guy is just plain doomed.)

- Any person other than a bona fide teacher of the English language who uses the word "parse" in public. See also Level Three for politicians who use the word. 0-1, 0-3, 1-1

- Hotel maids. As distasteful as this task is, I guess we have to deal with it. In spite of all the good work that hotel maids do, they are remanded to Level One because of the way they make up the beds. Their sin is simple: they tuck the top sheet under the mattress so that when you try to get in bed you must pull the top sheet out from under, which means you get the bottom sheet as well, which means you have to remake the whole bed, or just leave it flapping and wind up either wound up and tangled in the mess about two AM or with it all lying on the floor at the coldest part of the night. I was patient for the first 200 times this happened to me, but then I broke and assigned the poor souls to Level One. 1-1 (For more about the hotel maids' bosses and the designers of hotel rooms, see Levels Two and Three, respectively.)

• People, usually southern belle types, who compliment everything, no matter how boring, trivial, trashy or utterly miserable it is. 0-3, 1-1, 1-3

• Excessive smiling (it doesn't take too much of this to be excessive, either) 1-1, 1-3

THIS PAGE FOR LISTING OTHER LEVEL ONE RESIDENTS

Level Two

BOORINNNNG AND TRASHY!

Here's the drill on the folks who qualify for Level 2 (Seriously serious):

- 2-1 cause a whoppin' lot of minor irritation;
- 2-2 cause major irritation;
- 2-3 cause others to carry out one or more Level 1 sins
- 2-4 minor damage to the earth
- 2-5 actin' on a seriously out of whack idea about who or what is God
- 2-6 Minor liar
- 2-7 Cause serious trouble by acting stupid
- 2-8 Acting hateful
- 2-9 Utter tastelessness

The very title of Level Two gives you an idea of who might qualify to go there (along with the failed Level One people, of course). Level Two absolutely adsorbs people who have spent significant portions of their lives being better than others and telling the others all about it. Superior people. These people have managed to advertise their superiority in many ingenuous ways. Along the way, of course, they have done some serious sinning, and—simple jerks that they are—they are proud of it, and want to tell you all about it.

When it comes to advertising one's superiority and thus spreading boredom, word of mouth has been a standby, using loudspeakers whenever possible, but even the whispered word has been used to create its own level of intense boredom. The written word has been widely used, through both hand-circulated documents and published works. Signs have also been used extensively. Body language has been used. Messages have been tied to small dogs. Your own experience will recall for you some of the novel approaches to boring other people that have made it possible for the inventors and users of these cunning methods to arrive at Level Two.

People who are aiming for Level Two have to be careful to avoid what we hellions call "overshoot". If the content of their discourse rises beyond the boring and trashy to the hurtful, Level Three is possible. An out-of-control bore seldom achieves level Four since a true bore usually doesn't have the brainpower to be dangerously or viciously harmful. However, they can do it by mistake and sheer bad luck, so don't think there are no bores in Executive Level. Also, it is well to remember that you can be a bore and an SOB at the same time. In other words, just because you are boring you aren't totally safe from lower levels, so don't start bragging about the fact that you are only going to Level Two.

- Telemarketers. Of course, the inventor of telemarketing from a phone bank is in Level Four. 2-1

- People who leave the icicle decorations hanging from their eaves after May 15. 0-1, 0-2, 0-5, 1-1 [Stuff] Good Heavens! These people were only supposed to be in One, but what can you do? Rules are Rules.

- "Christian Businessmen" who tell you that's what they are. 2-5

- Litterers 2-2, 2-4

- Graffiti artists. The graffiti-for-Christ group goes directly to Level Three. How anyone could think that defacing someone else's property would be a good enticement to join his or her religion is beyond me. And I've tried to figure it out. 2-2, 2-4, 2-5 (graffiti-for-Christ only 2-9) [Stuff for g-f-C only.]

- The person who invented "lite". This one has been a hard call because Level Three beckoned. In spite of that siren call, after much thought and as a matter of mercy, the person who invented "lite" will be spending the rest of his days (Surely no woman would have been guilty of this?) listening to eager inmates tell what it was like last nite when the moon was just rite, giving out a perfect lite under which a person in a fite, if he were real trash, mite bite everyone in site. This will go on long enough to give even a person with a lite, sparkling personality a world class case of digustation. It is going to take a whole lot of good, solid, functional HEAVY to erase the amount of lite that has been let loose on the English language. 1-2, 2-2, 2-3

- The first subdivider, or the publicity hack therefor (and this one could have been a female), who added an "e" at the end of "Town Point Valley" to turn it into the infinitely more desirable "Towne Pointe Valleye", started something awful and deserves to be punished for it. I don't know when this started, but I'm thankful that it isn't the Wilbure Crosse Parkwaye, or Parke Avenue, or Palme Beache. Thank God there is no Chicagoe. (Yes, there is still a lot to be thankful for in this world.) For this "genius" and his or her followers, who have gone on to create Founders Pointe, Sturbridge Pointe, Johnson's Pointe, Weste Pointe, and every d***e kind of Pointe imaginable, not to mention Farmes, Glennes, Parkes, Endes, and other numbing e-words, Level Two has opened its arms. And they are going to stay open for as long as it takes to get all of these geeks out of the gene pool.1-2, 2-1

• The "e" thing made me think about the unfortunate sadist who first figured out that you could attach to a magazine such things as cards, thick pages, sniff tests, and other trash that keeps you from flicking through the pages. He is here in Two only because of an extraordinary act of mercy. It really is a Three offense. 2-1

• Oh, and by the way. the magazine art director who decided to leave off the page numbers from eighty or ninety percent of the pages so you can never turn to anything—even if you can find it in the crazy and confusing Table of Contents with little pictures that look interesting but don't seem to apply to anything (particularly the highly touted cover story that is listed in the contents under a title that seems to have nothing to do with the teaser on the cover). Oh well, at least we can be confident that they will all enjoy Hell—there's no table of contents there, but they'll keep thinking there must be one on the next page. 2-1

• People who agree you to death in order to get their way. The Southern Woman is particularly good at this. A truly excellent practicioneress simply cannot be resisted. 2-1, 2-6

• Tailgaters. 2-1, 2-7 (the ones who drive, not the ones who eat)

- Failure to use your turn indictor is a Warning item, however repeated failure is a ticket to Level Two. So far, no one has been able to fail at this just once. 2-1, 2-7

- Hotel housekeepers are in Level Two because they are the ones who tell the maids to tuck the top sheet under the mattress so it won't hang down below the bed spread. They are, of course, also the ones who tell them to stuff the extra roll of toilet paper into the recess behind the "duty" roll when both rolls are still full so they are jammed so tightly that you can't get the duty roll to roll. 2-1, 2-3

- All lawyers who aren't in Level Three are in Level Two. Thanks for asking. 2-2, 2-3 (could be 2-6, 3-1)

- Speaking of lawyers (see above) and bureaucrats (OK, we weren't.) How much do we really have to be protected from ourselves by an over eager bureaucracy propelled by more defensive- and offensive-minded attorneys than there should ever be? Consider the following scenario (a real life drama):

  You can't remember the name of the physician who performed a certain (unmentionable in a family book on Hell) procedure on you a few years ago, and the GP who referred you has retired so you can't ask him. You want to have fun again, so why not call the hospital where it was done and just ask? Seems simple. Get a handle on your social security number, your date of birth, your blood type, your mother's maiden name, your major credit card number, your phone number, your address, your mother's address when she used her maiden name, your astrological sign, your zip code (I know you have already given that in your address, but this is a new question.), your minor credit card number, your auto and homeowner's insurance carriers' names and the policy numbers, and any other little trivial number (like your bank account number) you think those in power might want.

Then, dial the hospital phone number. After three or four levels of automated answering and button pushing, you get to talk to a person. Then, another person. Then, another person. Tell the third or fourth person to whom you speak just what simple information you want, give them all the numbers they can think to ask you for and Presto! The friendly clerk tells you that she can't release this information to you, even though you have told her everything there is to know about you except your proctologist's report (let's face it, that's who you are trying to get in touch with). It's hospital POLICY.

But there is a simple solution: they will send you a letter with a return form enclosed, to the probably fabricated address that a vicious punk like you has made up solely to deceive them and gain valuable personal information about a person you claim to be but aren't. Just sign and return the form saying that you agree to have the name of your doctor released to you. They will then check with their lawyer, and if she agrees you will receive the reply by return mail. Please allow four to six weeks for delivery.

Say! Why not call the office of their advertising agency and ask for a list of the proctologists who practice at Mammothe Communitye Hospitale. They will send it in a flash and you'll recognize the name when you see it. Greed does conquer all, even bureaucracy. Why didn't I know at the beginning of this mess that I was going to have to call the PR people, and just do it in the first place? I guess hope does spring eternal. (Go ahead, call me a hopeless romantic.)

Even though the PR crowd provides a happy ending to this story, the bloody trail that had to be traveled to get to it qualifies the poor hack who dreamed up that POLICY for a seat in Level Two. 0-1, 0-5, 2-2

- The person who got the idea of putting a sign in front of his church so a new trivial saying could be displayed each week. Level Two really isn't deep enough for this guy, but Three is pretty crowded at this point. 0-1, 0-2, 0-3, 1-1 [Stuff]

- Architects who "make a statement" with their new building in a historic preservation area. The statement that is made is almost always inappropriate and the Hell of it is that we have to look at their miserable statements until they finally get knocked down. 2-2, 2-4 (could be 3-5)

- The inventor of shoes with pointed toes for women—or for cowboy boots, for that matter. 2-1

- Finally, we get to the designers of hotel, and, of course, motel rooms. When writing a book about Hell, it is most fun to write an entry such as this right after you have been victimized. The whole subject is so much fresher and exhilarating, and you know in your heart, as well as in your mind, that there is a place in Hell for them. I always like to start with the bedside lamp. It is NEVER high enough to allow you to read in bed. As far as I can tell its only real purpose seems to be to give you enough light to see to turn the light off. That's not really as dumb as it seems, although it is pretty dumb. If there are two beds, the cheap places where I stay have only one light fixture located between the two beds, so in addition to being too low, it is also too far away.

This level of planning and execution is so impressively fine! It absolutely requires you to sit in a chair to read, which is probably better for your character. And since the other lamp is not near the comfortable (well, not really that comfortable) chair, you get to drag the chair across the room. Another bonus. You can drag it back right before you notice that the clock has been screwed to the bedside table facing forward so it is impossible to see the time from either of the beds. Are we in Level Four? I hope so.

I don't think we can give the room designer credit for thinking to leave off the little slip of paper on the telephone that tells the phone number of the hotel—but whoever did do that is somewhere here in the crowd for that offense, and for at least two or three other offenses as well.

Hey! We haven't even gotten to the bathroom yet. (I know that we mentioned the toilet paper roll in Level Two, but that wasn't a design flaw.) What about that mirror! The top of it is only 5' 9" above the floor, so if you are over about 5' 10 1/2" you can't see to shave or apply your eye makeup or brush your hair without bending over. And that showerhead: it's a real sweetie-pie-only-sixty-inches-high. Really great for washing your hair if you are a midget. But, hey, it gives the height-enhanced among us another chance to bend over for a while. Enough of these little opportunities and you might be able to suffer permanent damage to your spine.

I did go to a motel once where the cunning designer—probably to leave room for an HVAC duct—had lowered the ceiling over the bathroom counter top enough so that if one were foolish enough to use the lavatory to wash one's face and were crazy enough to think that one could actually bend over the bowl to rinse so the water wouldn't drip onto the floor, then one would hit one's head on the low ceiling unless one remembered to step back two paces before straightening up. One was really in a mess in that one. In fact, with any luck at all, one could hit one's head twice the same morning. I am the first to admit that not all hotel bathrooms are designed this cunningly, but I like to give short designers full credit for their work whenever I can.

I wish the Hotel Bathroom Designers Protective Association had a published 800 number. If they did I would publish it again right here so you could call with your own little stories and suggestions. You could even suggest Level Four. Are we there yet, mom? 2-1, 2-2, 2-3

Raymond D. White

THIS SPACE FOR LISTING OTHER LEVEL TWO CREEPS

Level Three

LUXURY CONDO LEVEL

Here's how you can qualify for Level 3 (Bad serious):

- 3-1 leave a lasting hurt on someone else;
- 3-2 take something that ain't yours (goats, wives, and so forth)
- 3-3 bust something that ain't yours (goats, wives, and so forth)
- 3-4 adulterate with something that ain't yours (goats, wives, and so forth)
- 3-5 damage the earth in a significant way;
- 3-6 cause one or more persons to carry out a Level 2 sin
- 3-7 sass your mom or dad real serious
- 3-8 major liar
- 3-9 messin' up other people with your crazy ideas about God
- 3-10 makin' other folks work when they oughtta be smellin' roses (and you are probably just laying around while they are working)

The Merit Award people and the people in Levels One and Two can sometimes be dismissed with a grin or a shrug. We had rather they hadn't done what they did, and we may wish they just hadn't been on earth at all, or we might have been satisfied if they had just been somewhere where we were not, but the scars they have left are relatively slight and with time they will heal. Not so for the Level Three people. Level Three is for those who have progressed below mere irritation and have caused actual, lasting damage to other people or to the earth. The Level Three people have left scars that will remain forever on the unfortunate people or places that bear them. You can't laugh away a Level Three person and no shrug can undo the damage they have done. They need some serious Hell.

- The word "parse" has been discussed before, but it is important at this point to introduce the idea that use of this word by a politician is particularly egregious. Any politician who uses the word "parse" in public deserves extra depth in Hell—particularly if the comment has to do with a person, place, thing, event, idea, political or philosophical system, or anything else. 0-1, 0-2, 0-3, 1-1 [Stuff], 2-6

- Here's a big one: the people (I am convinced that there is a group who meet in a foul-smelling underground cavern to plot this stuff) who figure out the airline ticket rules. You might think that Level Three is a bit too deep for these people, however you must remember that at least 90% of their rules don't do the airline any good, they just irritate YOU. For instance, the idea of making a one-way ticket cost as much as or more than a round trip came from Hell, so it should just go back there. Another jewel is the idea that you can frequently buy a ticket to a place that is farther away for less than you pay for a ticket (round trip, of course) to a closer city. Then there is the "tar baby effect": once you have paid for this ticket, you can't get unstuck—it's yours forever. Use it or die. Of course it is not transferable; but if your luck is bad you can't change city pairs, and if you have even worse luck, you are required to travel in the same clothes you were wearing when you purchased the ticket. Don't laugh, they have a way to check this.

Now do you believe? 2-1, 2-2, 2-3, 2-7 [Stuff] Let's think about this. Level Four actually may be what we need here.

- Political speeches are almost always boring enough to rate Level Two for the speaker—and for the writer. Instant response by the other side always merits Level Two, and frequently gets Three. 2-1, 2-2, 2-3, 2-6 (could go to 3-8) [Stuff]

- The person who discovered that you can sell something by saying nothing about it and instead talking about the exact opposite. The combination of cigarettes and fresh air comes to mind. This may be a Level Four, depending upon what you are selling. 2-6, 3-1

- The guy who came up with the idea of turning up the volume during commercials on TV. The miserable flacks who put out the explanation that there is some technical reason for this are immediately behind the inventor himself in the seating order. 0-1, 0-2, 1-1, 2-1 [Stuff]

- The lowlife who invented the laugh track and burdened us with it, apparently forever. You have to admit that the laugh track keeps a whole lot of would-be comedy writers off the bread line, but the price we have to pay for that questionable benefit is just too high. I don't want to be told what is funny, I want to be convinced. 1-5, 2-1, 2-6, 2-9 [Stuff]

- Whoever started the rumor that alcohol is not a drug. 3-1, 3-6, 3-8

- Thieves, robbers, and burglars. 3-2

- Vandals. 3-3

- Adulterers. 3-4

- Actually, the largest single group of people in Level Three is telephone stock salesmen. They are as different from ordinary telemarketers as sharks are from goldfish. You know them: HELLO-MR-WHITE-HOW-ARE-YOU-TODAY? (At this point comes the only pause in the whole thing, and if you haven't already hung up you have to tell the rat that things were pretty good until he called.) Then you get: HI-THIS IS-BRIAN-GWALTNEY-CALLING-YOU-FROM-DI-VERSIFIED-CON.-I-DON'T-WANT-TO-SELL-YOU-ANY-THING-TODAY *(this last sentence is the absolute tip-off, in case you are innocent enough to have had any question in your mind heretofore)*-I-WOULD-JUST-LIKE-TO-SEND-YOU-OUR-NEXT-FOURCOLOR-BROCHURE-ABOUT-OIL-WELL-DRILLING-FUTURES-OPPORTUNITIES. Level Three really isn't low enough for these guys, but I don't know what else to do with them. 2-1, 2-6, 3-1

- The inventor of automated telephone-answering systems. You may think this is a little harsh, but I don't. I'm particularly interested in the thinker who made it possible to call, get the choice of dialing O for the operator or going to Mr. Blow's extension; I choose the extension and get voice mail. Blow is out of town for a month. They have cunningly made it impossible for me to dial O at this point, so my only current option is to leave him a voice mail message and wait a month for him to return it. Of course I could make another long distance call and dial O at the beginning of the whole thing this time. But, wait a minute. I have to pay for both long distance calls. There's something wrong with this picture. Still think the guy who figured this up is not in the right place? 0-1, 2-1, 2-2, 2-3 [Stuff]

• People who put up Christmas decorations before Thanksgiving. I can't decide whether this is worse in the residential setting or in the commercial setting. When I am in charge there will be a law against this. Hell isn't bad enough. Reminds me of my long-time Jewish friend, A. A. Freelund, who loved to intone "It absolutely disgusts me the way you Christians try to inject religion into a perfectly honorable commercial holiday like Christmas!" He was so right. 0-1, 0-2, 1-2, 2-5 [Stuff]

THIS SPACE FOR LISTING OTHER
LEVEL THREE GREASEBALLS

Level Four

EXECUTIVE LEVEL

This is it. The following offenses will ensure that you spend eternity in Level 4 (Over-the-top serious—no joking about it):

- 4-1 hurt a whole lot of people moderate-like;
- 4-2 hurt a bunch (less than a whole lot) of people real bad;
- 4-3 severely damage the earth;
- 4-4 cause lots of people to carry out level 3 sins
- 4-5 blasphemy
- 4-6 messin' up a whole lotta other people with your crazy ideas about God
- 4-7 makin' a whole lotta other folks work when they oughtta be smellin' roses (and you are probably just laying around while they are working)
- 4-8 ordinary murder
- 4-9 mass murder
- 4-10 all other really beyond belief bad stuff

It is difficult to find simple earthly examples that can convey just what eternity is like in Level Four. As I attempt to rise to the occasion, I am increasingly tormented by visions of my state legislature. It is a model that embodies many of the elements of today's Hell. The members of the legislature have struggled to get into a leadership role, but then sprain their necks ducking every time there is a tough question that demands leadership. They have only one true goal: to get reelected. The Hell of that is that reelection will simply require them to continue the never-ending struggle to duck the hard questions. They will have to continue groveling for cash and support from everyone they see. Then they will have to continue to act powerful—even though they may have a sinking feeling that they don't have enough power to blow up the balloon for a breathalyzer test. They will have to keep figuring out how to balance the demands of coming from all of the special interest groups that have bought their support for both sides of every issue. After all this the legislators get so tired (ashamed, maybe) of the hellish burden of it all that they retire. Only in Level Four they have to start over again, and again, and again, and again… I like it as a model for Level Four. Maybe you have your own favorite governing body. If so, feel free to think of it whenever you think of Level Four.

Even though thinking of your legislators in Hell has a jolly and quite satisfying feel to it, the legislature isn't quite bad enough for Level Four; it's a little too jolly in the legislature (the lobbyists do feed well). There is nothing jolly about Level Four. Nothing. It is Hell down there, and it is a Hell beyond your sickest imagination. Take your worst and cube it: Level Four is worse than that. When it comes to Level Four, we must remember that we are dealing with those who have hurt others, frequently many others. These were hurts that were bad when they happened, and that linger, and linger, and linger. Hurts that sometimes are visited upon the victims, their children, and their children's children—unto the fourth generation—or longer.

- Well, of course, Hitler is here. In the front row. Where the flames are closest, the fumes are smelliest, and the waves of liquid sulfur roll in regularly. 2-2, 2-3, 2-5, 3-1 [Stuff], 3-2, 3-3, 3-4, 3-5 [Stuff], 3-6, 3-8, 3-9, 3-10 [Stuff], 4-1, 4-2, 4-3, 4-4 [Stuff], 4-7, 4-8, 4-9, 4-10 [Stuff] (Please note that this is Level Four plus FIVE Stuffs. Only the most effective mass killer can do this.)

- Truly vicious punks. There used to be a lot of postal clerks entering this group every year, but this has changed since someone carelessly gave the Postal Service the idea that it is there to serve the public. It only took our postal service about 175 years to figure that out. However, in spite of the delay, it does prove that semi-free enterprise works! Not to worry. There may not be many postal clerks joining the line these days, but there are still plenty of vicious punks out there, so there won't be any unused seats in the vicious punk section of Hell. 3-1, 3-2, 3-3, 3-4 [Stuff], 3-5, 3-8, 3-10

- One of the most evil members of the telephone stock sales-men's cohort is here in Level Four. It's the guy who thought up the idea of having a recording call you—usually, in my experience at least—with a friendly massage from a political group that I wouldn't spit on to put 'em out if they were on fire. It is bad enough to get up from the dinner table to talk with a human telemarketer, but when it turns out to be a recording they have crossed the line, and it's war to the end. 0-1, 0-2, 2-1, 2-6 [Stuff], 3-1

- A significant fraction of the good folks rotting down here in Four are disgraced politicians and televangelists who have had the nerve to go back into politics or back on the Tube after their jail sentence is over and are trying to raise still more money or votes. We only owe them so much, right? So, after they have blown it all over us, why can't they just get a job like the rest of us once their jail sentence is over with? Really! How trashy can you get? 0-1, 0-3, 2-2, 2-3 [Stuff], 2-4, 2-5, 2-6, 2-9, [Stuff], 3-1, 3-2, 3-6, 3-8, [Stuff], 3-10, 4-1, 4-2, 4-6, [Stuff], 4-7, 4-10 (Please note that these lads—actually there are a few gals, too—are two sins beyond Hitler. Gives you something to think about.)

• Well! Ergonometrics! If ever there was a reason to send people to Hell, some of the more creative misapplications of ergonometrics qualify in spades. You can inflict torture on hundreds of people for hours at a time and do it again day after day almost forever with one misguided flick of the ergonometric switch. Which brings us to the people who design airplane seats.

The first ergonometrician (hereinafter referred to as SOB1) came to earth on a spaceship from an evil planet. He mated with an earth woman who thought he was just a lawyer and was willing to do almost anything for a country club membership. They had children, and all of the children were 5' 9" tall. That is where it all went wrong. SOB1 naturally assumed that all persons forever after would be 5' 9" tall, and decreed that as a cost saving measure everything in the future would be designed for a person of that exact height. The person of that exact height is known as SOB2, and ever since, all parts of airplanes and automobiles, as well as watertight doors on ships, and too, too many other things have been designed to perfectly mirror SOB2's elfin body.

It has been a bad run for the rest of us. If you are shorter than SOB2, you can't see over the top of the steering wheel and have to look through the spokes. (The new high-strength materials developed by engineers have been a godsend to short people by reducing the number of steering wheel spokes required.) On the other hand, if you are taller than SOB2 and are in an automobile either your head will touch the headliner, or the top of the windshield glass will be just below your horizontal line of vision, meaning that you can't see farther than the hood ornament unless you lie on your back.

Now we reach airplane seats. This is serious. Sit down for this unless you are in an airplane. If you are in an airplane please—RIGHT NOW—call for the smiling cabin attendant to restrain you (you can recognize them because they are all 5' 9" tall). Naturally we do not speak here of first class; we are speaking of where I fly: last class. That is where the seats are narrower than my shoulders. Statistically, of course, I do fit in this seat. At least, I keep telling myself that, and it sure makes me feel better in a statistical way.

It almost makes me forget that some SOB2 decided that each seat should have an integral, forward curving headrest. Not adjustable. Why do you need to adjust it? After all, everyone is an SOB2, right? No, not really. Those of us are SOB2+ end up with our rear ends firmly placed where the integral, non-adjustable lumbar support doesn't support us and our neck pinioned by the headrest with the full length of our back touching nothing. This makes the back hurt after a while, so we slump, and then both our back and our neck hurt at the same time. LEVEL FOUR IS NOT BAD ENOUGH FOR THEM.

It's tough all around, isn't it. But, we will get them. I'm thinking that we could have a little special place in Hell for the SOBs. All of the doorways just too low for a 5' 9" person to get through without bending over, all the steering wheels just too high to see over, all the bottom shelves just too high to reach, and so on and so on. And of course everything will be at metal melting temperatures with sleet or freezing rain around the edges. That won't be enough, but just knowing something is there waiting for them makes me feel better. 2-1, 2-2, 2-3, 2-7 [Stuff], 4-1

- National Association for the Advancement of Automatic Weapons (also called "NAAAW, man, naaaw", or NRA for short). Yes, the organizational awards continue. Some people would have you believe that anyone who would consign the NRA to Hell is anti-gun, that they want to prohibit all firearms. Nothing could be further from the truth. I am one of the dwindling group who believe that the Constitution meant business when it gave the citizenry the right to bear arms as part of a well-ordered militia in the service of the nation. I say let every citizen have his own single-shot muzzle-loading rifle and a similar pistol. It is a bit difficult to maintain a high level of rapid accurate fire with muzzle loaders, but that's what the founding fathers had, and it's what they wanted us to have, so I'm all for it. If the NRA would just join me in this approach, I could get them out of Hell, but as long as they have no confidence in the Constitution and continue to hold out for automatic weapons of mass destruction, they will have to stay in Hell. Pray for them. It is never too late for an organization to get out of Hell—as long as it is still alive. 4-2, 4-4, 4-8, 4-9 [Stuff]

- Leaders who don't lead. Why don't they just stay at home. Or maybe they could send a good, large dog to take their place. At least you could pat the dog's head and it wouldn't need an office staff and all the other stuff. 1-3, 2-2, 2-3, 3-1 [Stuff], 3-6, 3-8, 3-10, 4-3 [Stuff]

- All the other mass haters and killers are here. 4-8, 4-9, 4-10

- So are the regular ol' murderers 4-8

- Blasphemy. Dante assigned blasphemers to level seven, a pretty tough judgment, considering that there were nine levels. Having only four levels in our streamlined, environmentally friendly, fuel-efficient Hell, we are putting them all the way down in Level Four. This is done only because they deserve the worst we can do for them. We are not too worried about their sin against God, for God can handle things without our help. Our concern, and, indeed, God's concern as well, is over what the blasphemers can do to the "least of these".

  Who are the blasphemers of the day? Sailors who cuss like sailors are not included here. They are sailors, after all. Neither are the witches whose obituaries contain the obligatory witch-line "Although listed in the Social Register, she could cuss like a sailor when the occasion demanded— and it often did." These "shes" typically have a hard time getting below Level Two. Writers for and actors in TV shows and movies that are larded with dirty words are not here, either. They are mostly in Level Two based upon the boredom they have caused, and upon the dumbing down of the language that results from the extremely small vocabulary that they use.

  No, the blasphemers at the top of our list are the

wholesalers, almost all people who have power and position. Most of them have access to a TV network, a FAX machine, broadband e-mail, a high-speed copying machine, and a mailing list. There are a few poor souls who are forced—not withstanding their efforts to the contrary—to rely on retail blasphemy delivered only by the unamplified voice. We feel for them, but they are still here in level Four: incompetence is not rewarded.

The retail blasphemer is just as revolting as is the wholesaler whose words are borne on the airwaves to gullible millions. The only real differences are organizational ability, efficiency, charisma, and luck. Essentially the same things that separate a world class murderer like Adolf Hitler from the small time spouse murderer: the hate and madness are the same, it is just that some people are born to be masters and others are born to be simple journeymen, or even apprentices.

The blasphemer takes people's money. The blasphemer takes in the gullible and preys on the weak. The blasphemer uses people. The blasphemer hurts people. The blasphemer makes lives miserable and drives some to suicide, and even to murder. (How many killers do it because of some sick idea about God that was pumped into them by a blasphemer? And the blasphemer does it all in the name of God, and whenever possible at a good, solid profit. 0-1, 0-2, 0-3, 0-4, [Stuff], 0-5, 1-4, 1-5, 2-3, [Stuff], 2-5, 3-2, 3-4 (some of 'em, anyway), 3-6, [Stuff], 3-9, 3-10, 4-2, [4-3, Stuff], 4-4, 4-5, 4-6, possible 4-10, [possible Stuff],

Level Four Special Award

• I want to pay genuine tribute here to the wise engineers who developed the keyless entry system for automobiles. I love punching that little button and having the doors unlock for me. However, I do wish that please, please, you guys would get together and arrange all of the buttons the same way so I'm not always opening the trunk of my brother-in-law's car when I borrow it. Maybe the United Nations could handle this. Somebody needs to.

But I'm wandering. Back to reality where we are going to be speaking about the crumb who invented the gadget that makes the horn blow when you punch the lock button on the keyless entry for the second time. I understand that this is so you can tell whether you punched it for the first time. Wow! This ingenious device makes it possible for people who are too dumb to know whether they have punched a button to blow a horn so all the rest of us can hear just how dumb they are.

I have to admit that there is some good in this. The first time your new neighbor blows the horn, you are getting some good information about just how dumb and insensitive he is going to be for the next five or ten years. But after that first blow, every other one is redundant. And I am worn out with you people who blow your horns in parking lots (it's OK if you are trying to FIND your car). You can be as dumb as you want to just as long as you don't tell me about it. Will somebody PLEASE make these things against the law? I haven't decided whether the nit who invented this thing should be lower in Hell than the geeks who use it, so while I'm deciding, we'll just leave all of them to baste in Level Four. This just in!! BMW supposedly has developed a system that beeps twice. I don't know whether you have to punch it twice or whether it is two-for-one. Never been able to get that close to a BMW—just hear 'em bleating in parking lots. With luck, of course, your hand can get spastic and you can blow it four or six times!! Enjoy! Enjoy!—while you have the chance—because there won't be any of those gadgets in Heaven or Hell. 1-2, 1-3, 2-1, 2-3 [Stuff], 2-9, 3-6

- That reminds me of people who put gray-tinted plastic over their license plates. Please don't. It is against the law, and if God had wanted us all to have gray license plates She would have made them all that color. Relax! Just kidding! This is just a merit award. There is a related group whose members are in level two—the good folks who have their car windows tinted super dark. Two things: we really don't care who you are or what you are doing in there, and if you ever want me to let you turn ahead of me you are out of luck, because before I let someone in I like to see the whites of their eyes so I can at least get a vague idea that they are going to do what I think they are going to do. 0-1, 1-3, possible 3-1 (two possibles count as one confirmed for Stuff purposes) These guys, of course, are just in Level Three.

That's it for Level Four, at least until Volume Two comes out.

THIS SPACE FOR LISTING OTHER
LEVEL FOUR DIRTBAGS

RESEARCH FINDINGS: FIRST HALF

Original sin is looking great! Depravity is right in there! Paul was right on when he said that we can't even do good when we know what to do and that we can't even keep from doing bad when we know it is bad. Scripture has been upheld!

We have had some fun here, and we have also proved to a degree of certainty that I like to think would satisfy any hanging jury in the country that Hell positively has to exist. Where else is a good enough eternal landing place for all the worthy folks we have been discussing? And how about the grinding anger we would feel if we knew they were going to beat the rap, while we—who have been faithfully going to Sunday School all these years and have been drinking strong drink and giggling about it only secretly and while we are at church conventions far from prying eyes at home—weren't going to get something better than they get?

And how about the Hellbent theologians? They need love and affirmation, too. Life for them would be hell without Hell; it has to be there for us—but most important of all, it has to be there for them. In the First Half we have made it so. Our work here is done.

THE SECOND HALF

*Within Which Hell is Considered
Based on the Nature of God*

BIBLE STUDY TIME

The idea that God is sending us all to heaven seems to The Washed to be unscriptural. The washed feel it just isn't fair that the unwashed, who have lived their lives as sinners, will end up in the same Heaven that the well washed Sunday School Class members of The Washed are going to. But in spite of the long held Hellion belief in Hell, a belief that seems to have been nurtured by scripture, could it be that there is room in Heaven for everyone, even according to our own Bible, and could it be that Hell doesn't have a scriptural basis?

We have used the scriptures to explore whether there is a place for Hell, so now let's use them to show that Hell doesn't fit into the universe of the God of Love. What about—

God is love.—I John 4:16

Here's some real bottom line stuff: this makes it quite clear just what God is, and we can also figure out what God isn't: God isn't justice, retribution, righteousness, power, control, majesty, strength, and a lot of other things we have made Her out to be. (God does indeed embody these virtues, but scripture does not tell us that God is these things.)God is love—this would also seem to mean that love is God. If God is the ground of all being and God is love, then love holds everything together. That's something to chew on. This is my favorite part of the Bible.

In the beginning was the Word, and the Word was with God, and the Word was God. He was in the beginning with God; all things were made through him, and without Him was not anything made that was made. In Him was life, and the life was the light of men.—John 1:1

This is my second-favorite part. This is where we find out that God loved us from the very beginning and that salvation was part of the plan from the very beginning, too. Love/salvation (or is it salvation/love?) is God, and we just can't get away from God (see below), so we can't get away from God's grace which gives us God's love in an effective form (love that really does the job for us). The Word (AKA, love/salvation/Jesus) is what made everything and what holds everything together—there is no way to get away from it, and it has been there all the time. I like it.

For judgement is without mercy to one who has shown no mercy; yet mercy triumphs over judgement. (emphasis added) —James 2:13

You might call this the ultimate trump—the ace. You could also call it the perfect anti-catch 22, but what ever you call it, thank God for it. If anyone ever needed mercy, it's people, and God, being the thoughtful chap He is, has mercifully taken care of us.

All peoples on earth will be blessed through you.—Genesis 12:3

Notice the "all" part. Consider also that a blessing that would leave 161 billion people (and counting; see pretty far below) in Hell isn't much of a blessing. We can rightfully expect God to do a superior job of blessing—one that doesn't leave all those folks in Hell.

I know that you [God] can do all things; no plan of yours can be thwarted.—Job 42:2

This is another comforting bit of information. It is nice to think that grubby little folks like us can't thumb our noses at God and just tell Him we aren't accepting His grace and He can just like it or lump it.

Where can I go from your Spirit? Where can I flee from your presence? If I go up to the heavens, you are there; if I make my bed in the depths [of sheol], you are there.—Psalm 139:7-8

We just can't get away from grace. This is another case of our not being able to thumb our noses at God. Isn't it graceful that God set things up this way? Praise the Lord.

The Lord is good to all; he has compassion on all he has made.—Psalm 145:8-10

There's that "all" thing again. Thank God—again. (Presumably this makes a positive difference for us.)

For I am God, and not man—the Holy One among you. I will not come in wrath.—Hosea 11:9

Many people cling to the idea that God does come in wrath (remember that "A WRATHFUL GOD IS WAITING FOR YOU" sign), but this scripture clearly says He will not come in wrath. It relieves my mind.

I will pour out my Spirit on all people. Your sons and daughters will prophesy, your old men dream dreams, your young men will see visions.—Joel 2:28

God keeps doing good stuff for "all people". Of course, this kind of thing is no surprise when you remember that God is love.

God did not send his Son into the world to condemn the world, but to save the world through him.—John 3:17

"The world" sounds pretty all encompassing. Thank God. And do remember that The Word has been with us from the very beginning—it did not wait until 1 AD (or CE) to arrive (see above)—and will always be with us to the end of the earth.

When I am lifted up, I will draw all men to myself.—John 12:32

"All" again.

I did not come to judge the world, but to save it.—John 12:47

I guess this means what it says. Looks like love is in charge here. Lucky for us (see below).

All have sinned and fall short of the glory of God, and are justified freely by his grace through the redemption that came by Christ Jesus.—Romans 3:23

Just looking around convinces me that this scripture is right on (see The First Half). Looks like we would be in deep trouble without grace, but God knew that all along and took care of us. Remember the fact that Christ is not just a 32-year phenomenon; redemption began at the get-go (see above). Oh, by the way, here's the all thing again.

You did not choose me, but I chose you.—John 15:16

Once again God makes it clear that we don't have any thing to do with getting chosen: God chooses us—all of us—for eternal life with Her, and what God wants, God gets. All we have to do is enjoy it, and the sooner we start enjoying, the better. PS—you can't enjoy it unless you know what it is all about, which is why you need to be spending time in Sunday School. PPS—wouldn't it have been nasty of God to chose some people and not others, like the Hellions would have it?

I am convinced that neither death nor life, neither angels nor demons, neither the present nor the future, nor any powers, neither height nor depth, nor anything in all of creation, will be able to separate us from the love of God that is in Christ Jesus our Lord.—Romans 8:38-39

If none of those things can separate us from God, it is hard to believe that we—miserable worms that we are—can separate ourselves from God. Grace has saved us all, whether we want it to or not. And that's the final judgement.

God has bound all men over to disobedience so that he may have mercy on all men.—Romans 11:32

When we fell upward from the status of fox terriers we did become open to disobedience—and we do know how to be disobedient! Of course, when God gave us the chance to do good, God knew we were going to mess up more often than not, and went right ahead and made the final judgement that we were all going to be saved, whether we had messed up or not. That's having mercy and meaning it.

Love never fails.—I Corinthians 15:22

Amen! It is so comforting to know this. Of course, this means that God never fails, which we would expect from a God who was worth his stuff, and we were told in Job 42:2 that God is worth his stuff.

This is good and pleases God our Savior, who wants all men to be saved and to come to knowledge of the truth.—I Timothy 2:3-4

There is "all" again. In spite of everything the Hellions say, I'm beginning to be pretty sure that God really does mean "all" when She talks about salvation. We also have (see above) good authority for the fact that what God wants, God gets. It is of interest and comfort to know that our coming to knowledge of the truth is important to God. God wants us to know as soon as possible because the sooner we realize we are under grace, the sooner we can bask in that knowledge and the sooner we can start living like people who are the beneficiaries of God's grace. That's a good reason for spreading the Gospel.

...that we have put our hope in the living God, who is the Savior of all men, and especially of those who believe.—I Timothy 4:10

There's God again, saving all men—and we will assume all women as well. It looks like we get saved even if we don't believe (thank you, God), but if we do believe, we get the benefits of grace sooner (see above). That makes sense—grace is a lot like God's gravity in that respect.

[the Lord] is patient with you, not wanting anyone to perish, but everyone to come to repentance.—2 Peter 2:9

Here's God again, loving every one of us and planning for all of us to wind up in Heaven—and planning for all of us to be repentant—later if not sooner. (And we know that God gets what God wants.) God is some dude.

Giving God His or Her Due

Having done our arduous work in the First Half, and having proved without a doubt that Hell has to exist, and having just done our Bible study to prove that Hell and the God of Love have nothing in common, we now have to give God Her due. Some people tend to spend a whole lot of time trying to figure out what the nature of God might be and why she is that way. We, however, will reveal God with merciful brevity. No nine hundred page tome of small type for us. The truth is, if you have a God who can't be explained in a few carefully chosen paragraphs, you've got a God who just plain isn't cooperating, and that's not the kind of God we have.

For a start, we are going to declare that God is Love. The idea that God is Love is scriptural (I John 4:16), and even if it weren't, a God who created everything and then turned out to be so dumb He couldn't figure out that the only way to go was to be loving would be too dumb to take seriously. If the Big Guy actually had it in for us and was sitting up there in Heaven enjoying banging us around—or at the very least getting a kick out of watching us screw up—it would be such an impossibly uphill battle for us that we might as well just quit. The option of a mean or dumb God just won't fly. I could be a better God than that. So could you. And neither one of us would want the other one (let alone one of the Washed) to be God, thus we cut to the chase, go along with scripture and opt firmly for the God of Love.

Having a God of Love, we need to take the time to consider whether Hell fits in with the character of a loving God. We need to decide whether the wonderful construct of Hell that the Hellions have created and have come to need and to love is fair to all concerned, makes at least a reasonable amount of sense to the victims, and is something God will be proud of at the end of the day.

In order to satisfy ourselves as to whether Hell meets the above criteria and can be a part of a loving God's plan, we will once again join those who are convinced that Hell is out there waiting for us: we will start from the Hellion point of view and we will analyze Hellion Rules For Getting Into Hell to see if their rules really do a job a loving God can be proud of. We will proceed as follows:

We will test the rules under which eligibility for Hell is determined. Hellions are serious about the rules under which other people go to Hell, but they are a whole lot more serious about figuring out how to get around the rules so they can avoid getting sent to Hell. We will examine those rules, subjecting them to technically based scrutiny, including the unrestricted use of logic and irony. The use of logic is going to seem mean and petty to a lot of folks, but there is just no logical way we can not use logic. I know the use of irony will seem cruel and blasphemous to Hellions, but examination of these rules begs for irony and it would be cruel not to give Hellion rules what they deserve—and it is our considered opinion that Hellion rules have nothing to do with God, so there is no possibility of blasphemy.

We are going to be drawing lines in the sand and finding out whether the Hellion rules put God on the right side of the line, or whether God ends up looking like a jerk. If any rule makes you giggle after we have analyzed it, it is an automatic loser.

Then we will wrap everything all up into a brief Engineering Report that establishes once and for all whether Hell exists or not.

In case coming to the conclusion that Hell really isn't there after all surprises us, we will then use the Third Half of this book to justify all of the time we have been spending in Sunday School. Has it all just been a colossal waste? Should we have been reading cheap novels instead? Have we been suckered? Is somebody else getting away with something? Have we missed out on a doing a lot of bad things that we could have gotten away with? What do we do next? After these questions are considered this book will come to a polite end.

Remember, in this part of the book we are going to scrutinize and deconstruct the Hellion rules for getting into/out of Hell with the nature of God in mind, not from the Hellion's point of view.

In Genesis we read that "God saw everything that He had made, and indeed, it was very good" (1:31). That, of course, was in the beginning. When it comes to the end, and God looks back on what She has done with and for her creatures—including us—we want Her to have that same sense of deep satisfaction. We want Her to be proud, we want Her to feel like She has been fair, and we want Her to feel like the whole thing has made sense to us—and to Her. And, of course, She, too, wants to have all of those same warm fuzzies when She looks back on the day's work. It would be pretty sad to have created and operated an entire universe and then to find out in the end that you have blown it. This type of result would by particularly unfortunate if you happened to be God.

As we consider Hell with God in mind, we will keep asking the following five simple questions:

1. Is Hell really a practical alternative?

Could God just do something else for our eternal edification and be a whole lot better off from an environmental standpoint (all that smoke, all that noise, and the bad smells) and from a cost standpoint (Hell is not cheap to operate).

2. Is God (using Hellion rules) being fair to us?

Am I going to be unfairly sacrificed by being sent to Hell forever so somebody else can go to Heaven forever? Somehow that just doesn't seem fair. We expect all but the sorriest denizens of earth to be fair; one of our measures of the worth of a human being is whether he or she treats others fairly. (How many times have you heard it said about some disgusting gorilla—or homiletics professor— "He was tough, but he was fair…"?) Being fair does cover a goodly number of other sins. The least the Creator God could do is to be fair.

Wrapped in majesty divine, does God get to set up rules that we cannot, for the love of God, see to be even remotely fair? No. That will not be allowed on our watch. The God of Love is going to have to act loving, and that includes the lesser virtue of fair. It is sad to believe that some people think so little of God that they are going to end up being surprised if they find out that God really is fair to us. We will see.

When it comes to Hell, you are either in or you are out; there can be no half way. Some would argue that purgatory is the exception to this, but purgatory, if we were accepting the idea that it exists, would have to be a place for one to be purged of the last of one's sin so one could move on to Heaven. Allowing a final chance at cleansing does seem fair, but when the final cleansing was all over you would still get to Heaven unless you somehow managed to fail the course in purgatory, and ended up in Hell. When God makes the decision as to whether we are going to end up Heaven or Hell, we are going to expect God to be fair. Nobody will be sacrificed for somebody else because of some heavenly plan that we can't understand and that doesn't seem fair.

3. Is God's system (Hellion version) making sense?

Here's the logic thing again. I know logic will grate on a lot of you, but we simply must use it. Surprisingly, use of logic will get us into the Holy Mystery thing, and it may be that we will actually find ourselves getting into the Holy Foolishness thing. Hellion rules are based on the idea that God is the one who decides whether you go up or down (unless, of course, god asks you in and you just tell Him to stuff it as the Hellians seem to think you can), so we need to know how He is going to make that decision. Knowing, we can either avoid Him like we would avoid a pet shark in the swimming pool, or we can be sure to be standing in the right place at the right time with an ingratiating grin on our face and offer a shy wave when He comes by.

In order to get right with God—or to outsmart Him—we have to know exactly how He is going to make the decision about where we end up. There can be no fooling around here; there can be no gray area because you are going to be in or out of Hell for eternity. And there can't be any holy mystery to this, either, because I'll be damned if I'm going to Hell forever on the basis of some hokey-pokey mystery that nobody, including God's own elect, can explain to my satisfaction. If I'm going to Hell forever, I want to know why, and it has to make sense. Period. In fact, just for reference, I would even be passingly interested in knowing why you are going to Hell forever, if it comes to that.

4. Is God being efficient?

We are going to get down to engineering essentials and ask God to measure up to the same standards we pitiful humans set for ourselves. We expect a rather high level of efficiency from the pluggers down here on earth, so, when it comes to peopling Heaven, it seems that we should be able to expect some mind-bogglingly outstanding efficiency from the God of Creation. We'll see. We are assuming here that the God of Love's effort is directed toward peopling Heaven and not into seeing how many people She can send to Hell. Given the number of people whom we have consigned to Hell in the first half of this book, and the need a lot of people have for Hell to be out there, the idea that filling up Hell is not Job One for God may come hard to some gentle readers—but we aren't just making up this rule; the scripture does say that God our Savior "wants all men to be saved and to come to a knowledge of the truth." (I Timothy 2:3-4) So we have a right to expect God to be efficient and effective.

5. Does Hell make sense from a thermodynamic point of view?

You might wonder what in heaven's name thermo, and particularly its beloved second law—which we already know and love—has to do with this whole discussion. You are probably genuinely innocent of the basic role that energy plays in the life of—everything. Energy is, in fact, at the bottom of it all; without energy we wouldn't be here in the first place, and if we were here, we wouldn't have the energy to do anything.

You may also be innocent of the importance of moral energy. We will shortly be dealing with that lacuna, if it exists, in your person. Perhaps the appearance of entropy in a theological volume with the gravity of this one is just as much a shock to non-Hellions as to Hellions, themselves. But, bear up, at the famous end of the day we shall hope to be found to have given full satisfaction in the matter of the theological importance of entropy.

Rgarding The Nature Of God

Let's start our consideration of Hell from God's point of view by zeroing in on who God really is. We will begin by assuming that there is a God. Going through the debate on that issue is too much for a slender volume such as this, so we will save it for another time. (There are "paid hands" who are sweating over this right now, so don't worry that it isn't being handled.) For now, just buy it: God does exist. If you don't buy God, you are in the wrong book.

We will operate on the premise that not only does God exist, but that the Very God of Very Gods (our working version of God) is the only God out there and is the creator of the whole shooting match. The fact that God did the creating means that God was here from the beginning. This means that we do not have a God. Nor do they have a God. Presbyterians don't have a God, Baptists don't have a God, Christians don't have a God, and Muslims don't have a God. Nobody has a God, because none of us invented God. God really was here first. God invented us and God has us. [Note to alert reader: There are a lot of professional theologians out there who spend their time gazing at their navels and plotting out that we really do invent God. I'm not buying it: we do figure out our own versions of God, but that's not inventing, and I say God did the inventing.

God said "I am who I am," and sure enough, She is. God has real attributes, whether or not we know about them or accept them. Maybe they are not what we think they are, but whatever they are, they are. That means that God has a way, and that all the important stuff is done God's way, not our way. Thus, for this discussion, the Way question becomes: "When it comes to Hell, what is God's way?"

For me, the big question about who God is boils down to whether God is a God of power or a God of love. There apparently is a lot of comfort for the Hellions in knowing that their God can beat up my God, so they need a powerful God, one with all the latest equipment, accessories, and chrome trim. Thus, they have a God of power—and one who, in addition, is just. Presumably, the justice part is so the power part will be properly used, which is a nice idea. According to your Hellion, God is top-notch at loving, too, but only as long as the loving doesn't get in the way of the power and the justice. Our simple earthly justice system has as one of its tenets that it is better to let a guilty person off than to convict an innocent person. Apparently the Hellion God errs on the other side of the equation: fry 'em first and ask questions later. This is one of the aspects of the Hellion God that I have never been able to cuddle up to.

All my life Hellions have been telling me that God is all-powerful and that God is in charge of everything, has a Plan for it all, and that everything goes in accordance with that plan. My observations suggest to me that if God is all-powerful and is in charge of everything, He has really been messing up. I'm not sure whether it is a case of inattention, incompetence or downright meanness on God's part, but something just isn't working. In fact, a whole lotta things aren't working.

How could God let the holocaust happen if He really is

in charge, has total power, and has a loving plan? I can't come up with a satisfying answer for that. Of course there are a jillion other similar, if smaller, problems: birth defects, senseless murder, random acts of meanness, unbelievable stupidity (over and over and over again ad nausea), dynastic wars, and so forth. I can't come up with satisfying answers for those either, as long as God has the power and the plan. The effort to answer this type of question leads your Hellion to trot out "God has a Plan that we don't understand". This gambit may satisfy them, but my nonsense threshold is set a lot lower than theirs is, and my ability to suspend disbelief doesn't come near matching theirs. The fact that God-of-Power isn't working has been a long-standing problem for me because I have gotten an awful lot of God-of-power over the years. Some of my best friends are God-of-power people, and they seem well satisfied with that approach. Still, that idea is not persuasive for me.

I like to think of God as nice. Sure, God invented everything, and that was an impressive power-type move—and one that we need to be rather more than just a bit thankful for—but why did God invent the cosmos? That's where the nice part comes in: God wanted to give us a chance to be godly. The loving part comes in along with the nice part. As the scriptures tell us "God Is Love", which goes beyond God is "loving". The scriptures say that the essence, the very reality, of God is—love. As far as I can tell the scriptures never say that those other things like justice, power, vengeance, and so forth are the essence of God; they are just touted as being among God's worthy capabilities, for use when needed. So I like to think that when it gets down to the bottom line, the line is that God is love and the other good things flow from that. The other things do count for a lot, but they don't count as much as love. I know this is going to be unpleasant for some of you, but based on this analysis of God we are about to examine Hell and Hellbent theology using the idea that love is supreme—whether the Hellions like it or not.

Let's start our analysis by looking at an innocent little thing like the Rapture. I've always gotten a kick out of the Rapture—the bumper stickers are so good. It seems to me that for the Rapture to work, God has not only to extract the saved, if She is going to be nice about it, She has to bring all the unmanned cars (the ones that have those bumper stickers we mentioned earlier) to a safe halt and route the other traffic carefully around them. Naturally, the same thing will have to be done for airplanes, Amtrak, The Dog, and so on. This would seem to suggest, inter alia, that, since they are going to be here directing traffic, a lot of highway patrolmen and police officers are not going to heaven. This would also seem to suggest that as a safety measure all drivers or pilots of commercial vehicles should be certified unrepentant sinners who will be able to remain at the wheel during the Rapture. This is messy, and doesn't seem very nice of God, and as you know, I really am expecting God to be nice. Pleasant at the very least.

Of course, considering it from the Hellbent point of view, there is an alternate scenario: God may be planning to just let all the cars wreck. After all, why worry? Everybody left behind is going to Hell anyway, so what's a grinding car crash or two in the bargain? At least in this scenario the highway patrolmen and police officers would get to go to heaven. The salvation of the forces of law and order will probably appear to those remaining behind in the wrecks as a very small consolation, but it will be nice for the cops.

I'm thinking that maybe we don't need the Rapture after all. God can just leave it off. We'll get to Heaven another way.

Here's another problem: In spite of all of my early training about Hell and the Rapture, and all of the church signs saying "A WRATHFUL GOD IS WAITING FOR YOU" that I have driven past, [Note to alert reader: Remember this is not made up. I have actually seen this one.] my early inclination and the passage of the years have both given me reason to wonder about whether a merciful God would consign a soul to Hell (forever) just because of a simple failure to acknowledge a particular Savior. Generally speaking, in fact, a Savior that that particular soul had never heard of. In addition to the unfairness of it all, the thought occurred that Hell would have gotten to be an uncomfortably crowded place by now, and at the rate we humans are multiplying the crowding will be absolutely out of hand within just a few more generations. It was to sort out this type of dilemma that I began this probe of the unholy grail, Hell itself, thinking all the while, "What would Jesus do?" We will now ask some questions about the rules for getting to Hell—or for staying out of it, but first we will consider The Great Survey.

The Great Survey

Having established that God is love—for present purposes at least—we will continue our ramblings not by going directly to the Five Big Questions, but by considering a rather remarkable happenstance, tailor made, as it were, for our very purposes. That happening was the Great Survey made by the Baptists of Alabama. Perhaps you remember hearing about the survey yourself—or maybe you actually got surveyed. They carried it out a few years ago in order to figure out how many Alabamians (sp.?) were going to Hell at that particular time. I got the word on the survey from our daily newspaper, which has a penchant for reporting really important news just like this, always with big, juicy headlines, and hopefully with a picture of some blood. In this case there was no blood, but it turned out there was plenty of anguish in store for about half of Alabama's population. [Note to alert reader: in addition to my newspaper, *The Nashville Tennessean,* and a good many others that I don't know about, this news appeared in the Birmingham *News* of September 5, 1993. I did not make this up!!]

The results of The Survey seemed to hinge largely upon whether or not you were a Baptist, and it turned out that something like 46.1% of the whole population of Alabama were not Baptists or the full theological equivalent, and that same percentage were going to take a long, deep, hot, and totally permanent dive. Think what the percentage would be like in Idaho where the Baptists may be pretty thin on the ground. (Actually, I don't know for sure that they really have people in Idaho, let alone Baptists.) If Idaho doesn't excite you enough, how about Cambodia, or Peru, or Ethiopia, or Milwaukee? You are getting the picture, right? The worldwide Hellbound percentage is going to be high—really high. Scary!—particularly if you aren't a Baptist from Alabama.

The hellbound percentage (46.1%—keep it in mind, for it will be referred to again) doesn't just raise our blood pressure, it raises a number of issues we need to explore.

The Baptists must have gotten a lot of flack about the survey, because they shortly issued a "clarification" saying they weren't positively saying that all those folks were going to Hell; the Baptists were merely trying to figure out how much money to put into the evangelization line item of the budget, so they needed to get an idea of how many souls they needed to get out there and save.

Now, on to the five big questions.

BIG QUESTION NUMBER ONE
The Practicality Thing

Think of the practicality of the whole Hell thing. There's going to be crowding in Hell, serious crowding. You might even call it world class crowding. Not a pretty thing--unless you are just downright trashy and don't have any aesthetic taste at all. Maybe unpleasant body odor at close quarters just doesn't bother you. Maybe you just don't care about crowding in Hell, but even if you don't care, we can't just let something that important go, so we are going to think about this problem; we are going to treat it seriously.

Look at the results of the Great Survey from the Devil's standpoint. How can you torture effectively and efficiently when there's not enough room anywhere in Hell to swing a cat (let alone a sinner)? Face it: that just won't work. And if Hell doesn't work, who wants it any way? Not me, not God, and certainly not the Devil.

You might think you could trump the size problem in Hell by arguing that the doomed souls could be put into a very small place, like the small place occupied by the large number of angels that have in the past been proved to be able to dance on the head of a pin. Such ideas are refuted by the powerful but simple fact that it takes room to suffer. You have to be something to suffer. You can't have painful bunions without having feet to have the bunions. You can't burn in Hell if you have nothing to burn. In order to have a satisfying amount of serious suffering, Hell has to have space, lots of it. The fact that the Baptists have identified so many people—in Alabama yet—who are going to Hell creates a major space problem for the Devil, and it speaks directly to the impracticality of Hell. There simply isn't going to be enough room to have a workable and effective Hell. Urban sprawl will look like a Sunday School picnic compared to the way Hell will sprawl if it is just let loose. Hell, under Hellion rules, would have covered the whole Western Hemisphere by now and would be heading for Bangkok at flank speed. In a universe with limited resources Hell just isn't practical.

In addition to the space problem created by the requirements of a first-quality Hell, consider the operating cost: burning that much fuel to roast that many sinners for eternity would cost an infinite amount, and it would cost it at a high rate of expenditure. Not even the Devil has an infinite budget for fuel, and we haven't even talked about the cash flow problem he has because of having to pay the infinite salaries of the infinitely guarding guards. Once again we can see that Hell just isn't practical, and God wouldn't get us into an impractical eternal mess. In fact, He wouldn't even get the Devil into that kind of mess—nor would He let the hapless Devil get himself into that kind of mess.

BIG QUESTION NUMBER TWO
Is God Being Fair About Who Gets Sent To Hell?

In addition to worrying about a bunch of not-so-good people going to Hell (a low-grade, chronic worry), I worry about the "good" ones who have never heard the Gospel (a high-grade, acute worry), and therefore could hardly be expected by a just and righteous God, let alone by a loving one, to believe in said same God or savior. Is sending these "good" folks to Hell forever really fair? And then there are those, good or not so good, who have gotten the Message in such a backhanded or casual way that the only way they could have believed would have been due to

87

grace alone. And for some reason God didn't give them grace! What about them? Are they responsible for God's failure to give them grace? It won't work to try to claim that God gave them grace and they didn't accept it; God is in charge. Period. And what about God? Why didn't God give them grace? We might come away with the idea that God is playing an active part in sending people to Hell. Is that what we should expect from the God of Love? I don't think so.

From the Hellions (at least from a few of them), the answer to that problem comes right back, loud and clear, "Oh, not to worry: God takes care of the good people in pagan lands." Well, great. That is nice of God. But just how good do they have to be in order to get taken care of? Job made it pretty clear that he knew (and he knew that God knew, too) that we people aren't in God's league when it comes to goodness. When it comes to any really tough question we humans (Christians and otherwise) can usually come up with two exactly opposite answers, both based firmly in our faith, as to what is good, true, correct, or reportable. Let's face it, that's why we have a Congress. If we knew what was good for us we wouldn't have to pay 535 otherwise unemployed people to argue the questions for us. At least arguing is what they do when they aren't all clearly headed in the wrong direction. Yes, I have pondered the question of whether they are ever all headed in the right direction, and the answer is "Not often enough to count, or count on—particularly if the result has anything to do with my getting to Heaven".

So, if most of the time we don't even know what good is, it is pretty tough to make being "good enough" the basis for an honorable pagan getting into Heaven without grace. Is it grace that makes them good enough? Or did they get good enough on their own and are they being allowed to earn their way in because of grace? I'm getting confused here. Anyway, let's suppose that "good enough" is the rule. ("Good Enough", by the way is a well-used theological term that crops up in all kinds of weighty volumes on redemption, substitution, procrastination, and all sorts of similar stuff.)

In order to test this theory of being good enough, picture a guy in a remote village far from civilization as we know it. He has never heard of Jesus, but he has been a pretty good fella—really good, in fact. God is watching him and has him slated for Heaven because he is "good enough", but all of a sudden the guy—with no apparent provocation--smarts off to his mother-in-law and hurts her feelings real bad!

"That's it," says God, sadly, "That was one sin too many. He's off the Heaven Bound Train and is headed for Hell." Well, golly! Smartin' off at your mom-in-law isn't really a nice thing to do, but isn't it a bit much to send a guy to Hell for that, and forever, to boot? Okay, okay, maybe that one wasn't bad enough; we'll give him another chance. But, he's now got a REAL problem: no matter what he does wrong next, he's going to Hell for it. And the poor sucker doesn't even know it! Even the hardest hardshell Hellion at this point would say, "Well, it's a gray area," or "It would have to be a big sin." (At least I think this is what they would say, out of the love in their hearts. But then again, they don't want love to outshine justice, so maybe the love in their hearts isn't enough to allow them to step up and make a friendly offer like this.)

The problem with the Hellions' gray area is that there isn't any gray area (remember, NO neutral zone); you're either in Hell forever, or you aren't, even if you have to work your way through purgatory to get to Heaven. So that leaves us with the problem of the poor guy being done in by one big sin. A sin that's so big that you do one of them and you deserve to burn forever. And how big is that big? Still, some how, I just can't see a loving God popping somebody into Hell forever for just one sin, even if it's a BIG sin. To give the Hellion rules a fair shake, you might say that it wasn't just the BIG sin after the mother in law thing that got him, because if the mother in law thing hadn't happened, and he'd gone on to do a BIG sin, the BIG sin would still have been one short. You might argue that with no mother in law there would have been at least two more BIG ones, and that's true, unless some friendly murderer (say, maybe, his mother in law) got to him in time to kill him before that last fatal sin. But, even if he lived long enough to do two more BIG ones, eternity in Hell for just that last sin? Come on, God, give him a break. Any traffic cop in town would let him off with a warning. Surely God could be at least as loving as the traffic squad?

Would you send him to Hell forever for just one sin? I didn't think so. Wouldn't be fair would it? And frying him for eternity wouldn't be any fairer if God did it rather than your doing it. You wouldn't do it and God isn't any worse a guy than you are. (If you would do it, go directly to Hell. Do not pass go. Leave your money, your bearer bonds, and everything else behind.) At least, I sure hope God isn't worse than you; we'd really be in deep stuff if that were the case.

Here's another troubling little aspect of the problem. Let's say we have a really good villager who is slated for Heaven as a "good pagan"—top 2% of his class. He hasn't done that one sin too many. In fact he is a long way from the line in the sand, so he is a cinch for Heaven—if we just leave him alone. The last thing we want to do with this guy is mention Jesus. If we do and he doesn't buy the deal, he goes to Hell, and sending him to Hell is the last thing a good missionary would want to do.

Does that mean the missionaries should stay home? You could say "no" because since only 2% of the pagans are "good pagans", and with grace the missionaries' save rate could be over 50% for the bad guys in our remote village (remember Alabama!). Odds are that the missionaries would save a lot more souls than they doomed so it would be worse if they stayed home. Except, of course for the "good pagan" who was Heaven bound and gets everything snatched out from under him just so a bunch of serious sinners who happen to buy the message can go to Heaven. Still doesn't seem really fair for the good guy. This scenario also raises the question of why the good guy didn't believe when the bad (or at least worse) guys did? If it's "grace my fears relieved", why didn't God give grace to the good guy, and why did he give it to the worse guys? I dunno.

If the missionaries buy the 2% rule, think how bad they would feel every time they mentioned Jesus and the pagan didn't believe. After fifty of these, based on the 2% rule, they would be sending someone to Hell. If they could know who was in the 2% they could just leave them alone, but not knowing for sure who was in the 2%, should the missionaries just approach people who appeared to be really bad? This wouldn't waste any saves, but it would save the worst and leave the better, middle ground people to go to Hell. I dunno about this either.

All this speculation has been about the possibilities for the good people, and we know from scripture that there was only one good person, and, don't look now, it weren't and still ain't you or me. Are we wasting our time worrying about the good pagans if there really aren't any of them? What a tangle! This remote village situation is just too sloppy for me to be happy with.

Leaving the really good people behind, what about the villagers who aren't really outstandingly good, but are just average? Like us? We, because we live in Alabama or a contiguous area, according to survey results have a 53.9% chance of getting into Heaven through grace and evangelism (and, even though we are just average, our chance may even be a little better if the Baptists really get on the stick.) Using Hellion rules, the folks in the remote village have a zero chance to get to Heaven through grace because they have never seen a Baptist—and have seen only a precious few Presbyterians, although the Presbyterians do try— and, of course, it is no fault of the villagers that no missionary ever came to their town. So they are stuck. Well, actually they aren't stuck, they are on the road to Hell, and moving right along. Not so nice. Not so loving. Not very Godly, I'd say.

I don't believe that system works. I'm not happy with it. By, golly, I don't think it is fair. Who's in charge of salvation here? Get him front and center and let him explain this mess to me. I'm waiting.

BIG QUESTION NUMBER THREE
Is It All Making Sense?

General Musings

Being an engineer, I am not happy with something if it doesn't work. I am also wary of anything that doesn't make sense. I hasten to point out that this is quite different from being unwilling to believe in something that I can't prove. I can have faith, even if there is no proof. But what I can't do is believe in something that prima facie doesn't make sense and won't (and doesn't) work and for whose apparent lack of ability, utility, beauty, or caloric content there is no explanation that works for me.

You might reasonably ask why it is important for a nobody

like me to be able to make sense of a system that God, who knows and understands more than I ever will, created out of Her wisdom for my good. (At least I hope it was done for my good—and yours, too.) That is a good question, and one reason I should be able to understand the plan is that I may be just as important to God as are those well-known tiny sparrows, whose life and death are of such marked, and remarked upon, interest to a loving God. If I am at least as good as a sparrow, it follows, then, that my ability, and yours, to understand and successfully use the system God has prepared for us would be of more than passing interest to God.

You can also approach the problem of understanding God's plan from the operational side. Since God, according to scripture, set up this entire operation not just to allow, but, in fact, to encourage us to live the most Godly life that we possibly can and to get us into Heaven after that life is over, it makes very little sense from an operational standpoint to have a set of rules that are not intelligible to the users and that cannot be figured out on any logical basis. (I do understand that many, if not most, government forms are unintelligible to the user, and cannot be figured out on any logical basis, but you need to remember that it was in order to hold to a minimum just such anomalies as this that the framers of our Constitution made a clear separation between church and state.)

If God really cares about whether we are going to live a godly life, surely He would give us the tools to do so. We should be able to extrapolate the wisdom of the Bible from life in the time of the scriptures to life in our time. It ought to make sense. After all, we can't expect personal divine guidance (PDG) on every single matter that comes before us for decision or action. (Let's face it, we aren't televangelists. They, and their paying clients, are pros at PDG, we are just dirt–eating amateurs.) One spark of divine wisdom a lifetime wouldn't be a bad record for most of us, so we can hardly expect daily PDG—unless, of course, we are televangelists unaware and just don't realize our own eminence. So, THE INSTRUCTIONS AND THE GAME OUGHT TO MAKE SENSE!

The Prayer Thing

Sorting out prayer could be another whole book (I think there have been a couple already). We won't do the whole thing now, but we will puzzle over how we can expect prayer to work as far as salvation is concerned. Can we get to heaven on the wings of prayer—our own, or that of some concerned friend or paid claque? Can we expect God to listen to our every prayerful whim and then jerk creation around whenever we ask Her to in order to make reality fit in with our desires? The sort of confusion and commotion that would cause would be bad enough even if there were plenty of everything to go around, but it would be even worse in a zero-sum situation in which whatever we want to get will have to be taken away from someone else.

The zero-sum scenario, of course, assumes that we weren't going to get what we wanted in the first place, for in that case, we wouldn't be praying for it to begin with—or, at least prayer wouldn't be doing us any good. Taking what we want away from the other guy (unless, of course, under Hellbent rules he was one of the unsaved--sort of like the undead—who don't matter because they are going to Hell in the end anyway, and won't be able to shake their fingers in our faces in the hereafter because we will be in Heaven, ha, ha) doesn't seem very nice of God. The zero-sum looks particularly bad when you view it from the point of view of those people who think there are only a limited number of slots in heaven (around 144,000 by some counts): if you prayed yourself in, you would be keeping someone else out. Clearly, with about 175 billion people having passed through the earth (see The Event Horizon, below), the competition for heaven would be incredible and it would take an Olympic-class prayer even to get on the short list for Heaven, let alone get in. Prayer either isn't going to be worth a flip under those conditions or it's going to be a mean thing because it will hurt someone else—eternally.

Even if it isn't a zero sum situation and the other guy doesn't have to lose if I win, it still doesn't seem right for the most prayer-fully accomplished whiners to get the good stuff while the self-effacing get only the dregs. You might say "But you only get it if it's God's will for you." And I would then say "All right, then why pray? If it's God's will, it's going to happen anyway."

The reason we got off on this prayer thing in the first place is that an inordinate amount of prayer time has been spent on trying to get the recently—or, in a few hard cases, the long ago—dead into heaven. So, we must push on. The idea apparently is that the prayers of the pious are listened to especially carefully by God, and if you can get pious prayers in your favor you can overcome past imperfections (sins) and get prayed right up to the pearly gates—and on in.

This is "prayer for profit" writ large. Nothing penny-ante like praying for a better job or a new car or a cure for the heartbreak of psoriasis: this is big league praying and it is forever. What if the sinner who had the most prayer support from others could win with God? What if you really could get prayed into heaven? (Reformation alarm: this smacks of works, not grace!) That really doesn't seem very nice, since in addition to propelling an unfortunate class of grabbers into Heaven, it removes from God's care the very people who need God's love the most: the down and out, the alone, the helpless; those we would hope a loving God would be looking out for, and who probably wouldn't have a very big naturally-occurring prayer claque, nor the cash to hire one.

All of this reminds me of Cardinal Flavio Chigi, one of history's infamous Papal Nephews—Alexander VII was the Pope in this case. About 1680 the Cardinal caused a beautiful villa to be built for himself in the countryside near Sienna. The estate also included its own hermitage, high on a hill behind the villa. The hermitage was needed to house a corps of priests, or hermits, or whatever, who were on 24/7 duty praying for the Cardinal's soul. Seems the aspiring Cardinal Chigi had someone murdered in order to clear the way for his red hat, and he got a conscience attack after everything was done. Even before his death he had get-me-into-heaven prayers rising, and apparently he left enough endowment to keep them floating up for generations. I hope it didn't work. But, then, if he had just read this book he would have known that he was going to Heaven anyway. On the other hand, he would also have known that he would still be known as a murdering dog three hundred and more years later.

If the prayer system actually works the way the Hellions think it does, prayer doesn't seem to me to make sense, and on top of that it seems to be dazzlingly unfair. This problem may mean the prayer system isn't what the Hellions think it is, and God has created a system that is fair and that we can understand, at least as far as we are able to understand. It could suggest that Realprayer (TM; pat. appd. for; etc.) actually goes beyond fair all the way to the level of grace. Maybe there is no irrational, trendy, self-centered human jerking-around going on. Maybe prayer is not a way to get God to do things for us, but is a way for us to get in tune with God. Maybe—SHUDDER—prayer is LOGICAL. Maybe prayer makes sense, and maybe it works! It just doesn't get us into Heaven, God does that, but every good thing we do is an answer to prayer.

People do seem to mess up pretty much everything they touch—it's the sin thing. Of course, people aren't very logical either. Or at least they don't act as if they are. Actually, when you think about it, the world would work a whole lot better if there just weren't any people involved—but that's just too much to ask for.

In spite of the body blow to illogic that has just been delivered, you may not be willing to give up the divine guidance system that made America great (like English units rather than that horrible metric stuff). You may, in fact, still be tempted to claim that God does indeed give you divine guidance every time you ask for it, or at least every time She thinks you really need it, and that She will give the same to anyone else who earnestly prays. However, if you want to flog that particular horse, I would suggest that you look around at the rest of us, and back at history as well, and try, based on the actual results that you see, to figure out the percentage of people who have gotten divine guidance.

The human record of good decisions versus bad decisions suggests that either not enough people are asking (fervently) for guidance or that, ask though they might, they aren't getting it. There is failure here. You could almost say there's a Hell of a lot of failure. Whatever the failure mode, there are so many failures that we reluctantly (in this book, at least) reach the conclusion that that system of getting stuff by praying for it obviously isn't working. God may be sending out the guidance, but if He is, we have a pretty poor record of getting the message.

Why, after all, would God want to create a system (total

system, not just prayer) that doesn't work for the great majority of its users? Would you want to create a system for raising your children that was so incomprehensible to the children that they couldn't grow within the system? Of course not. Would General Motors want to create a system for making automobiles the workers couldn't understand? Of course not. Which leads us, falteringly and hesitantly, to the feeling that God didn't create the world system that way either. God must have meant for it to make sense, and it must make sense.

Let's pursue this further: we will assume that God does control everything. When asked why, if God is in control, the world is such a muddle, some would say, "Yes, it's true that things are a mess, but God has purposes that we can never know", or "God works in mysterious ways", or "Everything is a part of God's plan, and we simply do not have the ability to understand it now—we see through a glass darkly, but when we meet God in Heaven it will all be revealed." No doubt God does have purposes we cannot understand—our limited amount of smarts seems to be part and parcel of the state of sin. But if it is within our powers to know something, and that something is important to our lives, I have to believe that God has created the system in such a way that, within our range of ability to analyze, we can make sense of it. And, at another remove, the system should be such that our logic doesn't convince us of the exact opposite of the (supposed) truth. Surely God wants the whole thing to work out for us. He is a loving God, after all. The Bible does say "God is love," and, while it says many times that God is a God of justice, righteousness, and a lot of other interesting things, I don't remember it saying that God is those things. There is an important difference here.

Now we reach "conventional wisdom", and we need to look

out, because conventional wisdom sometimes does get things exactly backward. I would suggest that such often is the case because the conventional person often doesn't think about things at all, but just grabs hold of the first friendly or convenient idea that floats in through the window and feels good and has the smell of authority clinging to it. There is a well-known saying in engineering and architectural offices that "if you don't stop it from happening, the first thing that gets on paper will be the final design," and that seems to work in a lot of other situations as well. We need to test those designs and we need to test conventional wisdom—and what we think might be divine guidance—in order to try to make sure that they don't fly in the face of God instead of flying in Her slipstream. One way to test a situation is by analyzing it. We have only engineering logic to go on—after all, it is feelings that we are analyzing in the first place. [Note to alert reader: The preceding is the statement that the Engineer has been waiting for years to make, that he or she has silently nurtured through innumerable "feelings" sessions, and that God, Herself, has been begging us, for lo these many years, to get onto the table. It has happened. Selah.]

With all of this stuff rattling around in my head I started thinking (clearly a dangerous diversion) about the whole business of Heaven and Hell, salvation and damnation. Based on a lot of mental activity (perhaps it has a spiritual component as well), I have opted for Heaven and salvation. Some people say that they opt for the opposite, but I don't have it in me to believe them—unless they aren't in their right minds. Some others say they have never thought about it, and I guess that might be possible. That approach, though, does make me wonder if they have ever thought about anything at all. Maybe they haven't. For many of those who have thought about salvation, the answers they are being given by the authorities do not satisfy and the salvation issue seems to keep hanging around as a problem instead of a solution.

If salvation is an item at all, it is a big item. How many missionaries have been sent out to save people from Hell? How many sermons have been preached to save souls from Hell? How many earnest evangelists have worked cold and windy street corners with their Gospel tracts in hopes of saving from Hell the souls who walked by? How many radio and TV shows beam out over the ether to save souls from Hell? (OK, I know that most of them beam out to bring money in--but they at least started with the neat idea of saving people from Hell, and are they to blame if it turned out to be such a good idea that it sells?)

How does the hard working engineer attack the problem of Hell? Is there an efficient, theoretically sound, and empirically proven alternative to having all of these people in Hell? We will continue our analysis.

We Consider The Unborn and Others

What about aborted fetuses (aborted naturally or by human hand; doesn't matter which), and babies born dead? Obviously they haven't had the chance to make a "decision for Christ", or a "decision for Allah", or a decision for Whomever. So, does the loving God send them to Hell? "Well, of course not," comes the quick answer from the Hellion. "God takes care of those innocent little ones." (Techno-theo-logical explanation: they haven't reached the age of accountability, so God covers for them.) I find myself agreeing with that approach, since I believe that God's grace really is sufficient for everyone, and certainly would be sufficient for these innocents. However we got here, the Hellions and I are together on the idea that these little ones aren't going to roast. But we are still left with one or two reverent (or irreverent, depending upon your vantagepoint) follow-on questions.

The Abortion Question

The first reverent question is: Since these little ones have a 100% chance at salvation, and, according to actual survey results, the people of Alabama, whom almost anyone would hold to be a generally God-fearing group, have only a 53.9% chance to avoid the Pit, an abortion would actually give the average Alabamian almost twice the chance at salvation that a life would. Thinking in terms of eternity, abortion would seem to be the kindest thing to do in Alabama: almost half the people, who otherwise would have gone to Hell, would be saved.

Have we come up with the best possible argument for abortion? This may sound silly, but it isn't. We are, after all talking about eternity in Hell versus a mere three score and ten years on an earth that isn't unalloyed pleasure to begin with. It doesn't look like much of a choice to me: going for abortion is almost a no-brainer—that is if you are a Hellion. I'm still working on figuring out the flaw in my logic. Is there something here that doesn't make sense?

How Young is Young Enough?

The second reverent question has to do with those children who are born alive, but make it to Heaven under the Innocence Dispensation by dying young. How young is young enough? If you can get an innocence pass, the question naturally arises: "When are you no longer innocent?" Is it when you are two years old, or five years old—or twenty-nine years old in the case of a few late bloomers? Or is it when you have learned too much about the ways of the world? Or is it something else that pushes you over the line between a sure shot at Heaven and a 46%, or greater, chance to spend eternity in Hell?

Engineering logic and (hell) fire insurance considerations do not allow us to come up with a fuzzy answer to this question. "Oh, about four years old," won't do. Not if you are fixing the fate of someone who is 3 and one-half years old. I'd want to know precisely. After all, it's a pretty big thing to decide whether to dump the kid in the bag with the spare kittens and drop the bag off the Tallahatchee bridge so they can all go to Heaven for sure, or whether to wait another two weeks and see whether he gets saved. If I'm gonna dump, I don't want to dump a day late. Since we are talking about eternity in Hell for 46% of the troops, dumping seems to be an important option, one that we have to deal with. It won't work to try to say that the sins of the parents (the dumpers) will be visited on the innocent children. We have already established that they are innocent and that they will get a pass. So let's get specific: when are they not too young?

Maybe it isn't time that turns the crank, maybe it's knowledge that does the trick; the old apple off the tree of the knowledge of good and evil. So maybe we just shouldn't tell them anything. But deep in our hearts we know that won't work, because sooner or later they are going to find out about the birds and the bees in the rest room at school. What a dilemma! Do we let some kid at school drop little Johnny's odds on heaven from 100% to 53.9% on the basis of a casual chat at the moment we least expect it, or do we spill the crucial bits of news about life to the kid ourselves, and push him across the innocence threshold when we can be there to watch? Wouldn't it be neat for a little red light will go on somewhere just a few seconds before the damage is done? IN-COMING DAMNATION ATTACK! ALL HANDS TO BATTLE STATIONS! Brang Brang Brang Brang Brang... You could rush to dump the bag in the Tallahatchee before it's too late, or if you don't have the guts to do that, you'll at least know when to gear up and evangelize like crazy.

Let's face it, this whole approach has gotten crazy. It isn't making sense, but I can't see where else to go: the kids have to be humanized if they are going to be human, and somewhere along the way there has to be one single bit of worldly information that is THE one bit too much that puts the little one in danger of hellfire. Vagueness will not be acceptable. According to our theory, there is a line drawn in the sand, and if you cross it, your odds drop from 100% to 53.9% just like that. It seems like a pretty mean line to me. God created us humans, but as soon as She lets us go ahead and be human She puts on us the (probably best case) odds of a 46.1% chance that we will go to Hell forever. (This 46.1% figure, of course, is for Alabama where the Baptists did the survey to check. In the whole world, where the nominal Christian population is about 16%, and 46.1% of the 16% are going to fry according to the Baptists, the world-wide odds for a permanent trip to Hell go up to about 91%.) The truth is, I believe I'd rather not have come to the party if them's the favors that's being given out. I sure as Hell wouldn't bet if those were the odds.

The Mark Twain Factor
(Or How Long Is Long Enough?)

Frying a good guy forever for just one more sin (remember the guy in the remote village) looks even worse when you add in what might be called its opposite: the Mark Twain Factor. Twain theorized—just one of his many theories, most of them good— that Heaven must be full of murderers because his experience from attending as many hangings as he could wrangle a ticket to and reading about the rest, was that a very high percentage of the murderers seemed to get saved on the steps to the gallows. They might have lived a half-century as absolute devils, and might have been mass-murderers, but that thirty seconds of repentance on the steps to the gallows was enough for an eternal ticket to heaven.

Hey, wait a minute, what about the guy in the remote village? He was really pretty good—had to be a lot better than you or me (sort of like a woman who wants to be promoted at work) and he sure had to be better than a mass murderer—but he did just one too many things wrong (sassing his mother-in-law, yet!) and got Hell forever because of it. That doesn't seem fair to me, and fairness is one of our criteria! This whole scheme isn't working. It isn't making sense—AND it isn't fair. Once more, God is not looking too good. In fact, I think I see a trial lawyer who is more loving than to have put together a deal like that. Good God, what is the world coming to? I do see a trial attorney being kindly—there he is!

Twain's observation brings up another charming little question. This murderer repented thirty seconds before they hung him. How many seconds did he have to spare? Could he have repented just ten seconds before they offed him and still have made it to heaven? Good. How about three seconds, or 1/8 of a second, or a nanosecond. You can see how impossible this train of thought is getting. It isn't making any more sense than it was 30 seconds ago, and it was at the point of nonsense then.

You might say, "Well, this is silly, there has to be enough time for the guy to REALLY repent." Well, maybe so, but how do you REALLY repent, and how long does it take to do that? It happens that we don't have any sensible idea of what real repentance is, but if REAL repentance is involved, it is beginning to sound to me as if we have to work our way into Heaven, whatever REAL repentance might be. What happened to Grace? We are right back where we started from a few seconds ago, aren't we? And that poor guy in the remote village is still slated for Hell because of one bad mouthing-off at his mother in law.

This discussion of the fate of the murderer has been fun, but it hasn't been complicated enough. Let's throw in another twist: What if, as he was climbing the stairs to the scaffold, our murderer saw the chaplain at the top of the steps and thought to himself "Oh, good! He is going to have something to tell me that will save my soul!" Our boy is eager to hear what the padre has to tell him. He hurries up the steps and as his foot hits the seventh step, the step breaks under his weight, and he plunges down, hits his chin on the eighth step, breaks his neck and dies—just seconds before he was going to hear the words that would save him. He goes to Hell, of course, because he hadn't gotten saved. Too bad! Another fifteen or twenty seconds and he would have been saved, but we are working under Hellion rules and a miss is as good as a mile. He fries. Do you feel good about this? Is it working? Is it making sense for you? It isn't for me!

How Dumb Is Not Dumb Enough?

Okay, we have thought about how young is too young, which didn't seem to work, and we have thought about the Mark Twain factor, which could have been entitled "How short is too short?" which also didn't seem to work. Both presented major problems in that when examined in detail, the theories didn't seem to make much sense, or obviously weren't fair, or both. Now we are going to have to examine whether or not you can be dumb enough to skate past Hell and, as a corollary, whether you can be crazy enough to get a pass to Heaven. (Interesting: I've never heard the argument that you could get a Heaven Pass by being extra smart.)

Your compassionate Hellion would tend to resolve the dumb enough and the crazy enough issues on the side of fairness (your Hellion likes to think of God as fair. After all, fairness is part and parcel of justice, and we know God is just). Your Hellion would say that God would give a pass to people who were not mentally bright enough to make a decision for dinner, let alone for Jesus. Your compassionate Hellion would also be likely to conclude that if you were so crazy that you thought Jesus had just ridden past on a motorcycle with Eleanor Roosevelt in the sidecar on their way to root out the infernal devils who make chewing gum stick to the sole of your shoe, you probably would be crazy enough so that you couldn't be expected to make any rational decisions at all, and thus God would provide you with a Heaven pass.

These opinions are both thoughtful and compassionate. They do, however, raise the question of the line in the sand: Just how dumb or how crazy do you have to be to qualify for a pass? Let's cut straight to the chase: wouldn't it seem a bit ridiculous to send a gal to Hell forever just because her IQ was one point too high? Wouldn't it be even worse if her IQ had originally been below the cutoff limit for the Heaven-bound train, but had been raised just that one fatal point through the loving efforts of Christian (or Buddhist, for that matter) missionary teachers? It looks like having a "dumb" line is not going to work any better than the "one day too old" line worked, or than the 'long enough' line worked, or than the "Dead Before Arrival" pass worked. They didn't, and this doesn't.

The same problem arises in the case of the insane. Just how crazy do you have to be to get your free pass to Heaven? And if you are crazy enough, does it still work if you are "responsible" for your own craziness? What if your brain has checked out because you have abused drugs? How responsible for your sanity problem do you have to be to lose your pass to Heaven? Fifty percent? Ninety percent? Twenty percent? There are a bunch of problems here.

In order to save their eternal souls, should we be seriously worried about keeping crazy people crazy—enough? Should we be seriously worried about keeping dim-witted people simple—enough? And how much is enough? I don't believe God set it up that way, which means that either there are no dim/crazy passes (which doesn't seem fair) or there are no lines (which means everybody goes to Heaven—which does seem fair). Is there a dirty little secret out there? Can it be? Are we really all headed up? The evidence seems to be mounting. Stay tuned.

BIG QUESTION NUMBER 4
Is God's Plan Efficient Or Is It Wasteful?
(And What And Whom Is It Wasting?)

We are now going to enter the world of efficiency—the theological equivalent of running amuck. Together, we are going to re-engineer theology. Everything is being re-engineered these days, from the phone company to the Junior League, and the hell of it is that virtually no one uses an engineer to do their re-engineering. The present effort, at least, is being done by a real engineer, so we can hope that the God who emerges and the theology that describes Her, will be leaner, more loving, more efficient, and much more user friendly than previous nonengineer, ordinary human-concocted versions.

The liberal arts types—mostly art history majors, M Divs, psychologists, and sociologists—often say that God is extravagant, excessive, unlimited, warm, fuzzy, the author of process, and the very antithesis of a dry, efficient, results oriented (shudder) engineer.

The extravagance part seems to be true; the messy, convoluted and seemingly pointless nature of parts of the DNA chain is ample evidence of that. The excess part, too, is easy to agree with. Who but an excessive creator would ever have allowed the endless morass of TV (and radio!) talk shows that we have to put up with in order to get Masterpiece Theater or The Antiques Roadshow. Who, but an obsessively excessive creator could allow TV commercial breaks long enough for you to take the dog for a walk, brush your teeth, change into your jammies, water the plants, empty the dishwasher and fill the clothes washer all before the "show" comes on again? Talk about excess! How about the number of people on the earth? What about the number of unwanted domestic pets? The number of telemarketers? The number of televangelists? We could go on and on... Yes! Yes! God is extravagant.

God's creation does seem to be limitless: it encompasses fleas, tundra, wolverines, galaxies, tornadoes, micro-wave dinners, durable plastic combs, squids, elephant tusks, white dwarfs, gas turbines, anti-lock brakes, Monticello, Pilgrim's Progress, The Greenest State in the Land of the Free, sockeye salmon, verb tenses, sunset (every day!), art nouveau, grace, inflatable dunnage, Denali, Isaac Newton, Elvis, and on and on! There is no problem with the limitless thing, and it's neat!

Process seems to be smack in the middle of everything. The fact is that we don't know where we are headed on this earth—or beyond it, and wherever it might be, the way life is organized means that, like it or not, we spend our lives getting there, not being there. We need to be on the side of process, and we need to be working with God on the wonder of it all so the trip is the most fun it can be. Could it be that this whole "salvation" thing is a process that never ends?

There are, however, a few areas in which, in spite of our deep dedication to extravagance, excess, and the warm fuzzies, all of us, including the most liberal-artsy types one can think of, do want efficiency. We want results, we want them to be good, and we want them now—or at least real soon, and we all want those results. Even warm, fuzzy people want them. How about a messy extravagant desultory root canal? How about a ride on an elevator whose designer was more interested in the process of design than in the result of creating an elevator that won't let you down too hard? Want to be part of the "learning experience" of a thoracic surgeon who feels the world owes him a few failures so he can get to know how it feels to fail? I didn't think so. Me either. Those are some of the situations in which I want nothing but efficiency and results—good results.

I'm perfectly happy to give God a messy DNA chain, and I guess I can even gladly suffer through the dross on the airwaves—or turn it off. But when it comes to some things, including Hell, I want an efficient, results oriented God. After all, Hell is forever. We need to get God, Hell, and efficiency wrapped up into a neat, efficient package.

The Event Horizon

I like the idea of the event horizon—it actually gives me a warm fuzzy feeling. The event horizon has probably been employed in useful discussions by at least a million people, but the one who made it come alive for me was Stephen Hawking in his book *A Brief History of Time.* Here's a quick whiz at how it works: An event takes place, say the coming of a Christ, or a Muhammad, or some other divine messenger. The rules are that the event is the one and only event you absolutely have to know about and accept in order to be "saved". But what about the people who were "over the horizon" at the time and had no chance to know about it? This group includes the people who lived before it happened, or the people who could never, ever, have heard about it. Now don't give me that stuff about the guy in the remote village being all right, and that the people beyond the event horizon will be all right, too. We have already seen that that approach won't cut the mustard.

Let's carry out a crude little calculation to help us get a handle on just how many people are beyond the event horizon and therefor are, under Hellion theology, headed for a permanent berth in Hell. Here are the givens (Note: you can argue with any or all of these givens, but don't—let's just get on with it):

1. We will assume that the first humans appeared on the earth in 10,000 BCE. There are, of course, quite a few people who know that the first person appeared on a Friday in 4004 BC, and not a few others who think the first humans appeared at least 50,000 to 100,000 years BCE. For this analysis we are pleased to compromise at 10,000 BCE.

2. We will assume that a new generation of people arises every 20 years.

3. We know from checking the encyclopedia, that the growth of the population of the earth has been estimated to be something like this: no people in 10,000

BCE (our choice), one-half billion people in 1650 CE, one billion people in 1850, two billion people in 1920, six billion people in the year 2000. We will assume straight-line growth in between the points.

Using this information and these assumptions, a total of 166.37 billion souls should have passed through the earth by 2000. (This doesn't include all of the spontaneous—let alone planned—abortions, which would add tens of billions to the total.) We further assume that 16% of the world's population are nominally Christian now, and we will assume that the same percentage have been Christians since the year zero CE. (This is obviously giving an extra billion or so to the Washed.) We will also assume, based on the Great Survey in Alabama, that only 53.9% of the sixteen percent are real born-again quality Christians (RealChristians) [Trade Mark App'd for.] who will go to Heaven, and the other 46.1% are sadly deluded Presbyterians and Episcopalians who are going to be surprised to find themselves winding up in Hell along with the Muslims, pagans, Hindus, Zoroastrians, and others who muffed it.

A calculation based on the above gives us 3.77 billion RealChristians from the year zero CE (none before that) until the year 2000 CE, which means that only 2.27% of the souls passing through the earth have made it to Heaven. Put another way, there are 162.60 billion non-Christian and non-RealChristian souls in Hell.

Stop here for a moment and recall our discussion of the crowding problem in Hell. Also, consider our discussion about the need for practicality, efficiency and effectiveness in God's plan. Two point twenty-seven percent success is simply not a satisfactory record for a God who wants us up in Heaven. It wouldn't be a satisfactory record for a parachute rigger; it wouldn't be a satisfactory record for an elevator designer, or a bridge designer. It wouldn't be a satisfactory record for a surgeon, it wouldn't be a satisfactory record for a stock touter, or a horse touter, it wouldn't be a satisfactory record for a waitress getting food on the table rather than on the floor. The only human activity that I can think of for which 2.27% would be a satisfactory rate of success is direct mail advertising, or, perhaps, telemarketing. (The telemarketers, of course, all wind up in Hell.)

Can we honestly say that a loving God who created a system that has sent 162.60 billion souls to Hell to suffer for eternity while only 3.77 billion made it up to heaven with Him, has really lived up to His potential? Has He passed the efficiency test? I'm bold enough to say that I think not. God, Himself, would be ashamed of such a record, and wouldn't be able to defend it with a straight face in night court, let alone in front of Saint Peter or at a TV news conference. By the way, with the population base and growth we have now, those 162.60 billion souls in Hell are going to have a helluva lot of company just during the next century.

I am reminded of the statement attributed to Groucho Marx (and a lot of other people, too) to the effect that he never would want to join a club that would elect a reprobate like himself to membership. I believe I would feel pretty bad about having gotten into Heaven based on the ruling of a membership committee that created a set of rules that permanently set fire to 162.60 billion people so I could get in. Anyone who would be satisfied with a God who is doing such a sorry job really doesn't think much of God. I prefer to hold a higher opinion of the Deity. Really, if God couldn't do a better job than 2.27% saves, any one of us could take over and improve the situation. On a good day, a well-trained fox terrier could do better. Of course, if you are the type who just thrives on the idea of lots of other people going to

Hell while you, having heard the right things and said the right things, are enjoying Heaven, then a 2.27% God might be just right for you. Enjoy it while you can.

Even though some people may be happy to think that God is operating at only 2.27% efficiency, I don't believe that God is doing such a sorry job. I think we have an efficient God, one we can be proud of, and one whose stock or warrants I would be glad to peddle anywhere anytime. In fact, I think the job God is doing is so good that it is beyond human understanding or human love. She is getting 100% results, 24/7/infinity-that is, we are all ending up in heaven.

BIG QUESTION NUMBER FIVE
How Does Thermodynamics Affect God's Approach To Hell?

Dragging thermodynamics back into the discussion at this point may seem to be a major stretch, even for a self-professed engineer, particularly after all of the other mayhem we have created, but there are some aspects of thermo that we have not yet considered and that warrant serious consideration.

We have presented the argument that the Second Law of thermodynamics holds true for all systems including the moral system. We considered the Methodists and their battle with backsliding. Thought: What if the backslider had been backslid for just a nanosecond when the drive-by shooter killed him? Would he still go to Hell forever? In the light of our recent discussions that doesn't sound fair! Of course on a fairness basis we weren't any happier with the reverse idea of the serial killer getting into heaven after being saved for only a nanosecond on the gallows.

The seemingly random, and unsatisfactory, relationship between being backslid and being called to eternity is only one of the fascinating aspects of backsliding. Another fascinating thought is that no one seems ever to have had to worry about forwardsliding. When was the last time you worried about forwardsliding? The lack of concern about forwardsliding is where the truth of moral entropy comes even more clearly into focus.

Picture this: We are in Joe's Grimy Bar. There is a guy seated at the bar, a regular: complexion flushed, gut hanging out, nose red, eyes like two p*** holes in the snow. He is whining out his troubles to the bartender:

"It's just hell. I'm getting more and more organized. I've had a job for six months and I'm loving it. I'm on a diet. This beer may be the last one I ever have. I don't want to stop, but I just can't help myself. I have this incredible urge to help people, to be nice to them! The twelve Scout Laws are like a shining beacon to me; I want to live them all to the fullest. I've tried, but I just don't have the power in me to resist it. I want to stay a useless bum, but something is making me be good!"

The bartender is sympathetic, "I can't believe it. You've always been a scumbag. I'm shocked, absolutely blown out of my mind, to see a piece of garbage like you loose it. But, there's one thing you can count on: I'll always be here for you, buddy. You can come back and get drunk anytime. There are guys here who can help you get into any kind of trouble you want, any time you want. The door is always open to you."

You might say, "Well, this does happen. Forwardsliding is the miracle of God's grace at work." And you would be right: Forwardsliding must be a miracle, because it certainly isn't the norm. Forwardsliding is not what we expect, and it isn't something we can, or do, count on. When it does happen, we hail it, small though it may be, as the miracle it is. Forwardsliding is not an option that the damned can count on to get them out of trouble. Instead, morally we always seem to be ready to fall back into the chaos. The inexorable pull that we have to worry about is not a pull up to glory, it is a pull down to sheol. We don't give up and get better; we give up and get worse. We have to be on guard against backsliding; we have to fight the Ol' Debil. Theodore Dreiser's An American Tragedy was not about a guy who tragically fell in with church people and got good, it was about a guy who tragically went bad. Similar tragedies are happening every day.

Because we don't have to fight to be bad, but we do have to struggle to be good, you might say we are naturally hell-bent; that moral entropy is always increasing. Given the fact that we are so naturally hell-bent and that the Second Law of Moral Thermodynamics is always working on us, it is only fair that God should deal with this inexorable and disastrous process in a more effective way than by just dropping on us a salvation package that allows backsliding. Some people do think that once you are saved, you are saved for good—even though lots of other people are going to Hell—but that rubs me the wrong way because it seems like a Special, rather than a General, license to raise hell and get away with it. The idea of a general license (everyone goes to Heaven) has real charm, but the special license idea (only the lucky get an irrevocable pass) doesn't seem to pass the fairness test. In order to get around moral entropy, God has to lay on some serious grace and has to make it work, otherwise we don't have much of a chance at Heaven. Thank goodness She has laid on serious grace.

RESEARCH FINDINGS: SECOND HALF

Ion serious grace.

n the first and second halves we have used the Hellions' own system for deciding who is going to Hell and who is going to Heaven. The Hellions, of course, blame this system on God. Let's just recap where we have been and what we have seen.

- In the First Half we considered the need for Hell based on our experience with humankind and we concluded with almost no dissenting votes that Hell has to exist because of all the people we know who absolutely need to go to Hell.

Moving on to the Second Half:

- In looking at Hell with the nature of God in mind, we have found problems with the Hellion approach (which could be seen as the "God-of-Power" approach.) The God-of-Love approach, on the other hand, has been seen to have quite a few attractive aspects, and the God-of-

Love approach makes it very difficult to pin Hell on a God who loves us all.

- The Great Survey laid it on the line: only a modest majority of the people in Alabama is going to make Heaven under Hellion rules.

- Hell is impractical because of 1) space problems, 2) out of control operating costs, 3) smoke pollution and noise pollution (you know there's a whole bunch of screaming and yelling going on).

- When you take a serious look at just who and what we are, we don't measure up too well. It becomes easy to see that a system in which we earn our way into Heaven (or out of Hell) simply isn't going to work and that grace absolutely has to work if we are to have a chance at Heaven.

- The idea that God is going to send us all to Hell unless we have gotten the word and have been "saved" just isn't fair; it is also a massively inefficient system.

- Giving a Heaven pass to pagans who are really good people is a nice thought, but the whole idea falls apart when you start trying to decide who is good enough to make the cut and whether we might actually be hurting some "really good" pagans by telling them about Jesus and running the risk that they won't buy in and will end up in Hell because of our loving but fumbling efforts.

- There are important aspects of the Hellion system that just don't make sense, and if they don't make sense, how could the system do God or us any good? That being the case, we assume a system that doesn't make any sense is not God's system, but flows from the Hellions' own little minds.

- Getting prayed into Heaven, by yourself or by anyone

else, seems ridiculous, and the idea of getting prayed in by others seems, in addition, to fly in the face of God's love for those who are left out and don't have a prayer claque.

- The idea that the unborn get a pass and that the people of Alabama don't, brings us to the conclusion that abortion (a 100% chance at Heaven) is the solution to everyone's sin problem. This finding leaves us with an uneasy feeling, and doesn't seem to make a whole lot of sense, particularly if you are a Hellion who is opposed to abortion.

- Next we considered those who die young. They get a pass, which is nice, but then we had to deal with the question of how young they have to die, and that got us into the idea of putting the kids in the bag with the unwanted kittens and throwing them off the Tallahachee Bridge to make sure they got to Heaven.

- Then we ran into the Mark Twain factor: if you can live a totally rotten life and then get saved at the last minute—or half minute—and go to Heaven forever, how long do you have to have repented for it to work? We kept shortening the time and it kept getting sillier and sillier. It didn't seem particularly fair, either.

- We considered the feeble-minded and the insane. Giving a pass to both groups seemed to be a good idea, but, once again, we ran into that problem of where to draw the line: how dumb or crazy do you have to be to qualify. What if you contributed to your own problem? Is this approach fair to the people who just aren't quite stupid or crazy enough?

- We considered the event horizon, and concluded that if the Hellion theory holds, the system would be incredibly inefficient, would cause excessive crowding in Hell, and wouldn't be fair to the ones who didn't get the word.

- Finally, using entropy, we concluded that our natural tendency is toward Hell, and that God just plain needed to give us grace to get us out of an impossible situation (that She got us into in the first place.)

We have seen that, as much as we like the idea of Hell, Hell isn't working: it is clearly impractical, it is unfair, it doesn't make sense, and it isn't efficient. In addition to all those failures we have seen that moral entropy is inexorably sliding us toward Hell—and we had nothing to do with entropy, so once again, the system just isn't fair. Hellion grace seems to be floundering in the midst of this Hellion system. Hellion grace isn't cutting the mustard, but then neither is the rest of the system. It just doesn't seem to be the type of system that God will be able to be proud of at the end of the day.

All of this leads us to conclude that the Hellion system we have been examining is not the system of the God-of-Love who created us. It is, in fact, the Hellions' own system. It is a system they have developed over the millennia (there were Hellions BCE), one that they believe in, and one they have turned into a way of life for themselves. They have been telling us that God is behind it all, but we have clearly shown that God has nothing to do with this mess. We have looked right down the barrel of the thing and God is not in there.

Try as we may, we can figure out no reasonable, loving way to accept and explain the rules the Hellions are using to send people to Hell. So we are left with no place to send folks but to Heaven, and that seems to be just what a loving God would be up to anyhow (hint: we really don't have to do the sending after all; God has a whole different set of rules and the entire universe has been set up by the Very God of Very Gods not on the basis of power, but on the basis of love and grace that really works, whether your average Hellion likes it or not).

Shockingly (to some, at least), God is sending us all to heaven.

THE THIRD HALF

*An Attempt to Clean Up the Mess We Made
In the First Two Halves*

CLEANING UP THE MESS

The Sunday School Question

L ooking at things from the point of view of the God of Love, we have disposed of Hell, and now we are left with Heaven, which is a highly satisfying alternative. But just when you have doused Hell, have ample Heaven for everyone, and seem to be in a really good spot, some people immediately bolt and say, "Well, if there's no Hell and we are all saved no matter what, why have we been wasting our time going to church all these years? Why have we spent all those hours in Sunday School? Has it all just been a colossal waste? Should we have been reading cheap novels instead? Have we been suckered? Is somebody else getting away with something? Have we missed out on a doing a lot of bad things that we could have gotten away with?"

Good questions. Hell is a very important place if you think real life is not on this earth but is somewhere in the beyond, and Hell is a very important place if you think this life is just a vale of tears that is standing inconveniently between you and heaven. Hell is a very important place if you are concentrating on the "spiritual" because God is in Heaven—and we are down here on earth. Hell is a very important place if you believe God is a God of Justice and vengeance, and Hell is a very important place if you want God to take you away to Heaven so you can get out of dealing with the corner where you are.

In spite of how important Hell seems to be to many people, since we have gotten rid of it, our task in Sunday School is not to study Hell or how to stay out of it. We have to make sure we get clear about the fact that Hell isn't and the fact that God is. We have to spend Sunday School time getting at least a little bit of a handle on who God is and then we can concentrate on what God has in mind for us to do right here, right now, with the life She has given us. Life is what we have got and we will insult the God who gave it to us if we act like it is trash. Insulting God is not a nice thing to do, and the very least we can do is be nice to God. We might even go beyond nice and try to live the lives of disciples, and Sunday School can help us with figuring out how to try to live that life of discipleship.

The engineering logic on we humans is that while we may all be going to Heaven later, we can still be world class SOBs here and now, and we need to do something about the SOB problem. So we go to church to learn how to be more Godly on a day-to-day basis. How else can you be a good Rotarian? The truth is that virtue really is its own reward. Looking back on your virtues—modest though they might be—is not a bad thing at all. And, of course, your virtues will probably have caused you to do some good along the way.

On the other hand, if you have always been, and currently are, a world-class bag of dirt, don't get to thinking you are no longer dirt just because you have found out that God loves you—unconditionally. (Yes, here's the U-word, and this time we really mean it: unconditionally—absolutely without condition.) Nope, buddy, you are still a bag of dirt, and you'll keep on being one, too, unless you do something about it. Your sin may have been washed away, but the smell lingers on. The truth is, you probably need to be sharpened on one end and pounded into the ground like a tent peg—today. However, sharpening and pounding is a human game. We do it in history books, in gossip, on talk shows, in courts of law, in state prisons, and in many another way. And I think we should do it. Maybe if we are good about making the punishment fit the crime, and the notoriety fit the action, we will have a few less of those actions as time passes. (Rehabilitation is acceptable in addition to punishment.) God, however, has a bigger game to deal with than game of earthly crime and punishment. He has to administer eternal love—love that is beyond all understanding, so far beyond all understanding that it winds up sending everyone, no matter how bad and how unrepentant, to Heaven.

I know that some of you are thinking that Heaven could get crowded, too, just like Hell would if we use Hellion rules, and that a crowded Heaven wouldn't work any better than a seriously overcrowded Hell. But that is not the way it is. I Cor. 15:51 clearly tells us that we will be transformed when we go to Heaven to meet God. And part of that transformation might just be that we will become extremely small. I know the scripture doesn't precisely say this, but it is clearly implied (at least to those of us who speak regularly with God, so of course the implication is clear to you, too). There is a song that says, more or less, that "I could be as happy in one little room if you were there as I could be in a kingdom by the sea." If that is true for your average lover, I think we all can be happy in a teeny little space when God is there.

N.B.: soul multi-tasking will also be necessary so we can be all things to all people, which we will have to be if we want to be granny's little darling, a Metropolitan Opera star, a long-lost school chum, and a loving mother all at the same time for whomever needs what.

Even if you are going to end up in Heaven, you aren't there yet, so there's still plenty to do in Sunday School. This despite the fact that God loves you—or maybe it's because God loves you. You need to spend the rest of your life figuring out how to live as if you weren't going to Hell. Let's consider some of the things we need to work with in Sunday School.

Engineering Report on Hell, Executive Summary

In the first two Halves, we have managed to get ourselves into what is known among simple people as a "mess". Because we considered the situation from the point of view of human beings in our analysis in the First Half, it was actually quite easy for us to prove that there has to be a Hell because of all of the (un)worthy people who by their actions (thoughts don't count unless followed by action!) have unequivocally earned themselves a spot in The Burner. In spite of (or perhaps because of) the fact that we left God out of our work in the first half, we were unable to avoid positively swelling with pride upon contemplating all of those we have sent to Hell and what a good thing we have thereby done for the world and those who are still dwelling therein.

On the other hand, in the Second Half we have just as unequivocally proved that Very God of Very Gods, which is the only God we are dealing with (YOUR God is not in play, nor is MINE, OURS, or THEIRS), could never hold Her head up at the end of the day if She had created Hell and was operating it under Hellion rules. Furthermore, we have shown that Hellion

Rules Hell doesn't make enough sense to keep a saint or a sinner from giggling about it. We have shown that Hell is unfair, inefficient and politically incorrect (not environmentally friendly enough). As so often happens in theology, particularly the amateur brand, we have clearly proven both sides of the equation and have found that they are not only equal to each other, they cancel each other.

In order to dress them up and make theology about them seem pretty darned important, the gummy "messes" like the one we have gotten ourselves into are almost always called "paradoxes" when official theologians are puzzling over them. Some of them, in fact, actually are paradoxes, but most are simply the result of fuzzy or boneheaded thinking. The proper application of logic to the trains of thought that create a mess can usually bounce one train off the rails and leave the other one ready to roll on. We are going to do that. What we are going to do may seem to be simplistic and even brutal, but it is neither. Remember, the Hellion's God is not really God at all, but merely the Hellions' construct of God. Likewise hellion rules Hell has nothing to do with the Very God of Very Gods, so when we dump both hellion rules Hell and hellions' God we are not dumping on God or being irreverent to God, we are simply—but not simplistically—closing the chapter on some theologically aberrant behavior. It turns out that, using Hellion rules, we haven't been dealing with God at all: instead, we have been dealing with and have gotten rid of Anti-God and Anti-Christ. (This may seem extreme, but I believe it is true that the Hellions really are basing their theology on Anti-Christ instead of Christ.) As a result, here in the third half we are going to be able to deal with God and ourselves and we can use our Sunday School time to do that.

We may mess up when it comes to being loving, but God

doesn't. We may not be able to forgive our neighbor, let alone Hitler, Genghis Kahn, Saddam H., the terrorist called Xxxx and other highly successful murders, but thank goodness God can. God's kind of forgiveness is beyond our comprehension, but we are lucky it is there, and if we are smart, we will take it on faith. (If you want a little mystery in your religion, try that kind of love on for size.) The grace that the Hellions have concocted doesn't seem to work, but real grace, God's grace, does work, everywhere and all the time. We are dealing with the idea of truly unconditional love, which is hard to fit into human boundaries. Coming to grips with unconditional love is going to take a lot of Sunday School time.

We may think deep in our hearts that grace has to be earned, or at the very least has to be accepted before it can be effective. But God knows that a whole lot of us will never even hear about the Heaven-bound train or the ticket, and will never have a chance to accept a ticket, let alone get on the train. He also knows that not one of us is good enough to earn a ticket for the heaven-bound train, so God has made sure that His grace is sufficient for all of us—whether we know it or not, whether we accept it or not, and whether we like it or not. (If you want a little more mystery in your religion, try that one on for size.)

Let's consider which should weigh more heavily as we make the decision about whether or not to dispose of Hell: the human need for Hell or God's love. We will open the discussion by voting for God's love. Seems reasonable since He created this whole world, set up the rules, and breathed life into it. Of course we won't just dismiss Hellions and their ideas; they did give us the concept that "the God who loves you without qualification is going to send you to Hell forever if you don't happen to hear the Word or if you hear it and don't then say the right magic words".

That is impressive thinking, if thinking was involved at all. I confess that I do frequently wonder whether thinking actually was involved in that particular formulation. The Engineer has the feeling that there was feeling involved here; the engineer's feeling is that someone just jerked that idea out of the air—or from someplace else that he could conveniently reach. It is a good "Company" idea, one that can definitely scare a lot of people, give some others a good lifetime job of saving the first lot, and keep the Company in business. (I know that this is a bit mean spirited, but it is time to put the cards on the table.)

Once you get an idea like Hellion theology started, it is hard to stop it, but long standing Company Line or not, I have a hard time buying the love-you-but-going-to-fry-you idea of God (Hellion version). So in the end my vote remains for the God of Love—real unconditional love. We aren't going to let a bunch of Hellions say that God's grace is no good and kick sand in God's face, nor should we—even if some of the Hellions do have their own TV shows and even if they have run some of the world's very best inquisitions. It wouldn't be good for the gene pool to let the Hellions aggravate almost all of us to Hell (about 97% of everyone who has ever been on earth by actual Hellion-based calculation), so we aren't going to let 'em.

We are, at this time and based on the above rational nexus, once and for all dispatching Hell currently, retroactively, and forever. Getting rid of Hell has been downright fun and very satisfying, but this dispatching of Hell is going to be bone-crushingly disappointing to a lot of people. This disappointment is not going to be merely theoretical, it is going to be real. For some, the loss of Hell will pack an emotional shock, and for others it will pack a commercial wallop (keep the televangelists in your prayers). We owe it to those who are affected to deal with that disappointment, thus in the Third Half of this book we will contemplate what to do in Sunday School without Hell to keep us warm.

Bible Study Time

Well, here we are in Sunday School, and what else should we do but have a Bible study to get things going?

So faith by itself, if it has no works, is dead.—James 2:17

This is a verse that has been roundly condemned by those who think that we are saved by faith and not by grace. The writer of the book of James knew that we are not saved by works. He knew, too that we are not saved by faith; we are saved by grace. If we have faith in that grace, the proof of our faith will be our works for God—although those works, however strong or feeble they may be, have nothing to do with our salvation—neither does our faith.

Thou shalt love thy neighbor...—Matthew 5:43; Matthew 19:19; Matthew 22:39; Mark 12:31; Romans 13:9; Galatians 5:14; James 2:8

This looks like a pretty serious item in the minds of the writers of scripture. Maybe we need to be putting a lot of time and effort into loving our neighbors. Seems like God wants us to do just that.

My concordance of the scriptures has 16½ columns of closely spaced citations of the word "give". This makes me think there must be something about giving that is important to God and that we would do well to consider giving and do a lot of it if we want to live as children of God. Here are a very few of those citations…

Jesus said to him, "If you would be perfect, go, sell what you possess and give to the poor, and you will have treasure in heaven; and come, follow me." --Matthew 19: 21

…And the King will answer them, 'Truly, I say to you, as you did it to one of the least of these my brethren, you did it to me'.—Matthew 25:40

God doesn't need anything from us (God can hack it on Her own); but God knows that the "least of these" do need something from us, and we must try our best to take care of the least of our neighbors. Our faith can be "private morality" but, if we are not hermits, it must be "public morality" as well. If we fail in either of these spheres, we have failed God.

Give to every one who begs from you…—Luke 6:30

Pretty big job. We are going to have a hard time trying to live up to that one, but it looks like that's what we are supposed to do.

A new commandment I give to you, that you love one another; even as I have loved you, that you also love one another. By this all men will know that you are my disciples, if you have love for one another.—John 13: 34-35

This is a commandment that says "thou shalt…". It is a

statement of what it means to be a follower of Christ, and it is a very practical reality check: what you do is going to speak louder than what you say. We need to be sure what we do is done in love and what we say lives up to what we do.

We can study on these verses in Sunday School and we can find lots of other scripture that gives us at least a good hint of how God wants us to live and we can try to sort them out and live as God would have us live. That is going to take us a while.

BigJesus And LittleJesus

Size matters. Don't let anyone tell you it doesn't. One of the matters we need to discuss in Sunday School is to sort out whether we are going to go with BigJesus or LittleJesus. The prevailing official theological approach seems to be firmly planted on LittleJesus. As much as anyone else, we have Constantine to thank for this. He had an empire to run, and he needed a precise and exciting religion to help keep folks in line. LittleJesus was available and easy to understand. It probably helped matters quite a bit when during her visit to the holy land Constantine's mother came up with a piece of the true cross upon which LittleJesus was crucified.

Illogically (as I see it) we are being sold the Jesus of 32 years. The idea is being sold left and right that before Jesus arrived on earth the God of Love simply hadn't put in place any plan to keep people out of the Hell that moral entropy was consigning them to in wholesale lots. A few superstars like Moses, maybe, made it on merit, but that was so rare that for practical purposes (read: you and me) nobody was escaping an eternity in Hell. Then, after letting earthlings go for 4004 years, or a hundred thousand or so years, depending upon one's view of Bishop Usher, when

God did provide a savior, She had the nerve to require everyone to hear about Him, get the message clearly, and subscribe to it fully before letting them get on the Heaven-bound train, thus consigning billions more souls to Hell.

What a way to run a universe! As we have pointed out ad infinitum (almost) this approach hasn't worked, doesn't make sense, and isn't fair. Perhaps the fact that it is the ultimate "in group" approach to salvation is the very reason those in the in group have been able to suspend their disbelief in the incompetence, illogic and unfairness of their version of the "good news", and have been able to buy LittleJesus and keep right on selling Him to the next bunch who come along.

It is much nicer, easier, much more logical, and much more loving to settle on BigJesus, and accepting and selling BigJesus is one of the things we need to be doing in Sunday School. It is my contention that the writer of the Gospel of John know what he was doing when he started of with a discussion of The Word—The Word that always had been and always would be. BigJesus is the Jesus of the first chapter of the Gospel of John, the savior who has always been and who always will be. BigJesus is the Jesus who is at least as good as gravity (and maybe even better): works for us whether or not we know He is doing it; works for us if we haven't even heard His name, and works for us even if we have heard of Him but haven't acknowledged or accepted him; and works and works and works. BigJesus is the Jesus of everyone, the Jesus who is fair and who makes sense as one of the three parts of the God of Love. We need to work on being BigJesus people. BigJesus is the Jesus who brings us all (as in ALL) together as children of God, which makes a lot more sense than the LittleJesus who separates us into "the washed" and "the unwashed."

Messy Moral Issues And The Religion Business

Although some of us are tickled pink by it, the demise of Hell is going to be a big problem for a number of religious groups, and while we are in Sunday School we must deal with those groups—who are probably in Sunday School themselves. We will consider in Sunday School not the innocent followers, but of the leaders of these groups—the paid hands and the gurus. You can zero in on the groups that are likely to have the most trouble by following the bumper sticker trail. Look for the "In case of Rapture…" and "I have found it" stickers, and then find out who is behind them (actually, finding out which church the people in front of them are members of will probably be simpler—if you can get them to stop so you can ask). The religious businesses that are putting those stickers out have been counting on Hell to keep them in business for a long time, and it does not appear they are going to go quietly into that dark night where there are no innocents who depend upon them for salvation and are willing to send in their money to keep that salvation coming out of the tube. Business is business, after all. (We must admit that they (mostly) believe in what they are selling, even if we don't.)

Sadly, all too many organizations that were founded for the best of good reasons, and have done much good in their time—and are still doing a modicum of good—find themselves concentrating more on keeping the business going than on whether or not they really are doing enough good to justify the money they are taking in. Bureaucracy is bureaucracy, after all.

Of course there have been some religious organizations that have been founded for no good reason at all, but simply because the perpetrators came quickly to the conclusion that "preachin is a whole lot better than plowin, and I ain't gonna plow no mo' if I can hep it". Preaching can also beat selling used cars, sacking groceries, waiting tables, working for the man, and a whole lot of other ways to make a living that don't add all that much to the fun of life. The possibility of getting a much better deal out of life can put a lot of religion in a guy or a gal, and if they have what it takes to succeed in show business, they can usually memorize enough verses out of that limp-leather covered Bible to scare the hell out of enough people to develop a cash flow that becomes seductively satisfying. After all, there is a sucker born every minute, and the suckers don't spend all of their time going to the circus.

It is noteworthy that at times a certain "moral hollowing-out" takes place in some of our Churches (and other places of worship). This seems to have been going on since religion got organized, and lots of people have been sacrificed "for the good of the Church" over the years. Others have been run over in the street (literally and figuratively), have had their wallets cleaned out, have been enslaved, and have had lots of other dirty things done to them because they were unwashed and we Hellions were washed in the blood of the Lamb and knew what was best for THEM (after all, like the Lowells, we Hellions talk directly with God). Oh, and what would it hurt if we made a little money along the way?

The apologists for these whitewashed tomb religious groups have focused on sweeping their problems under the rug using the excuse that their "higher calling" of keeping people out of Hell justifies a few "moral lapses". After all, they are saving people from BURNING IN THE ETERNAL EVERLASTING FIRES OF HELL FOREVER, and that ought to be worth every cent the saved are sending in, and all of the other irregularities besides. Sadly—even tragically—this happens in large cap religions just as it does in mom and pop salvation shops. And it doesn't make it right no matter how many salesmen you have on the road.

If you are a religion-watcher it is a lot more fun to watch the mom and pop operations go wrong; they can be absolutely hilarious at times. The big operations, on the other hand, don't tend to be as funny, but when they go wrong, they make up in sheer horror for the fun you miss if you aren't watching mom and pop stuff. You can catch the mom and pop stuff on the tube, or right in your own neighborhood, but to see the big guys at their worst, you have to go to Chancelleries, Board Rooms, Lawyer's Offices, Concentration Camps, War Rooms, and such like. Most of us don't get to go into those kinds of places, so we frequently don't realize what the off-the-track large cap guys and gals are doing to us until ten to fifty years after the damage has been done. Most of the perpetrators are gone by the time we find out—and the hell of it is they have gone to heaven—so we can't get at them. The mom and pop operators, though, are right in front of us—in real time, as we say in the modern world—and when we see them messing up we can get instant satisfaction by attacking their tax-exempt status immediately. It is the American way; I don't know what they do overseas.

It doesn't seem to matter whether you are a big fish in a big pond or a big fish in a small pond, pond-power does have a way of corrupting all but those who are able to cherish and live by the dictum that the end does not justify the means. Those who have both gotten and understood (at least through a glass darkly) the Good News know that both the means we use and the good we do are what it's all about. The means is what we choose to use, and we must be sure that the means we choose are appropriate to children of God—who are trying to be godly. In order to choose the right means we have to seek God in the every-day, in the right here under our own nose, and for the good of our very own neighbor. There is plenty of Sunday School action here.

Getting souls to the "Kingdom Up There" is not our problem. When God was planning things out, He could easily see that getting folks to heaven after they have finished their time down here was too important a project to leave to village idiots like us, so He got that matter under control right at the get-go. Having taken care of the eternity thing, God has been gracious enough to give us the opportunity to make something good of this world— and Sunday School (wherever and whenever it happens) is where we need to be studying on how to use the right means to do a good job with this poor world.

There really is Good News. It is not new news, although it will be new to some: God really has loved you all along. God has not been planning hell for you, God has been planning Good for you. And, fortunately She has fixed it so nobody can get in Her way, which means you are going to get that Good in an eternal dose no matter how badly things down here get messed up.

The commercial religionizers and the religionizers who deal out terror from the bottom of their hearts would sleep a lot better if they could accept the Good News and start preaching it. No doubt the cash flow would decline, and some of them might have to go back to selling cars, but it would be worth it for the peace of their souls. After all, what does it profit a man when he gains a TV show of his own and loses his soul?

It is ironic—no actually it is just another paradox of Christianity—that while the real business of living the Good News is taking place, we aren't going to do the job of bringing the kingdom on earth, or at least we are never going to get it right, unless we have internalized the Good News. But, if we keep the Good News inside and are lured into making it a Me-and-Jesus thing that is devoted to getting us (me) into Heaven, it isn't going to do anything much for the Kingdom. We may walk alone the Walk with Jesus fast and furiously, but if we keep it to ourselves, in the end we will be found to have started off pointed in the precisely wrong direction. It is entirely possible that during our Walk we will wander into doing some entirely laudable "random acts of kindness" along the way, but we would do so much more for the Kingdom if we could just try to run straight toward the mark of loving others rather than having to get bounced into the right direction like some wandering pin ball with the machine constantly lurching toward "tilt" in order to get us going the right way.

We must accept that we do not seek a relationship with God to obtain His help to get our financial house in order, to get a better job, to conquer gingivitis, to find a good husband for our lovely daughter, to improve our complexion, or to conquer anything, so the religious operations that are offering that kind of payoff are sadly off the mark. It is hard to give up a good sales pitch like "Jesus can get it for you", but making that pitch is nothing more than whitewashing a tomb, so we must pray that all of those in the religion/moral leadership business who are using (and presumably believing!) "Jesus will get it for you" will give in and start using another pitch

Piety is laudable, but only if it gets outside our own skin and only if it leads us into serving others and living decently and lovingly with them. Jesus loving is good, too, but only for the reasons listed above. If you were the last person on earth there wouldn't be much point in being a Christian—God has already punched your ticket to Heaven, so Christianity doesn't do you any good toward getting there, and if there were no one else to be loving toward there would not be much point in—anything.

Fortunately, none of us have much of a chance of being the last person on earth, so the Good News of God, as demonstrated for us by Jesus, is the key to our living a life that rises above the lives lived by Dachshunds, lions, fleas, sparrows, and other similar creatures. If one doesn't live up to the Good News one can actually do a lot worse than the quadrupeds and the other -peds, and unfortunately all too many of us don't live up to the examples set by our dogs. We have a long way to go, but, thanks to God, with major assistance from Jesus, we can see The Way, so we at least have a chance to try and follow it.

The end-justifies-the-means type of activity that goes on in the name of God is not needed, won't pass muster, and, in fact, is the very definition of blasphemy. Never was the Lord's name used more in vain than in the name of religion. It is nice to think that the real Good News will come as a relief to some of the end-justifies-the-means people who will actually be free, and will no longer have to enslave people so "they" could hear the word of the Lord from one of "our" priests, will no longer have to betray people to the Nazis so the institution of the church could continue, will no longer have to cover up God-and-they know what dirty (big and) little secrets, and will no longer have to carry out other nasty tasks that may arise in the future.

The real Good News will come as a disappointment to people who have been charging more to the unwashed, or have been paying them less than they pay the washed, and have too good a thing going to stop. In order to get right with God, they are going to have to make some changes because it turns out that everyone is washed in the blood of the Lamb and we are all created equal before God and each other (Good grief, it looks like the Declaration of Independence was right!)

Some outfits are going to have to clean up their act, and

when things are cleaned up, all of the outfits can turn their efforts toward getting us to live as if we really believe God loves us—absolutely and unconditionally—and as if we want to embrace God in all that we do. Loving our neighbors as our selves is a job that we can work at for the rest of our lives. There's not enough Sunday School time available to get us trained up well enough to do a really first rate job, but if we spend some Sunday School time preparing ourselves, we can do a lot better job than we have been doing.

Some of this may seem to be a bit harsh, but it should be counted as tough love.

What About "Gotta Have Hell If You Are Gonna Have Heaven"?

Here's another Sunday School topic. Even though it has been a good seller over the millennia, idea of Hell needs a lot of propping up. One of the props is the idea that "we can't have heaven without having its [supposed] opposite, Hell". This one keeps cropping up—especially among more sophisticated Hellions. The idea that there must be an opposite is part and parcel of Hellion apology for Hell, and it is also used to prop up weak justifications for numerous other opinions such as poor taste in art, and bad ideas in general (the kind of idea that prima facie makes no sense and has to be pumped up with something that sounds sophisticated and unanswerable). The "opposite" argument sounds great in jacket blurbs, doctoral dissertations, and reviews of books on obscure poetry and dense theology, but like a lot of other important sounding arguments, it just ain't so.

In order to deal with the need-for-opposite argument, we are going to grasp and use the concept of "positive entity". We define a positive entity as something that exists in and of itself and does not depend for its existence upon anything else, including its supposed opposite.

Let's think about opposites: do they really exist? What is the opposite of a rock? Jell-O? Mud? Wind-blown pollen? Oatmeal? Paper or scissors? Well, what is the true and only opposite of rock? Kind of hard to pin down, isn't it? We could go on and on with similar examples, but enough is enough.

At this point, one might use the concept of matter and anti-matter to prove that everything does have its opposite and that according to the latest science, we can't even exist without opposites. I suggest that the anti-matter is actually not the opposite of matter, it is just matter on the other side of a divide. To put this in simple theological terms, if you were in another world and on the other side of the mirror standing the other way and looking out at this world, everything on this side would look the same to you as everything on that side looks to us, and it all would be the same except for the thin film of silver on the glass between us. There are no opposites involved in matter and anti-matter, just things looked at from one way and the same things looked at from the other direction. You could call it the blue crew and the gold crew. Besides, if you snap matter and anti-matter together you get nothing, which is not the opposite of anything special—it is nothing. (You can see that this is a rigorously scientific approach to evaluating anti-matter, but it does have charm in spite of its lack of rigor, and it does end up with nothing not being the opposite of anything, which is where we want to be.)

Let's move on to a more advanced concept: contentment. Do we have to have its opposite, discontent, in order to be content? (Or is pain, rather than discontent, the opposite of contentment?) Do we need a good dose of pain in order to know when we are not in pain and be thankful for it? I say we do not. I have been discontent, and know the difference between content and discontent, but I have not known all kinds of pain or all kinds of discontent, and the lack of that knowledge does not blunt my freedom from pain or my contentment. In fact, based on what I have heard about some problems and pains, I am more than a little glad that I haven't been able to partake of them. While there may indeed be a lesson to be learned from some particularly noxious kinds of pain and discontent, I am happy to remain ignorant; if there is character to be built, I would as soon have my character improved by another method—or just limp along with the character I have. Of course, if you want some additional pain or disaster to further improve your character, I know a guy who would be glad to break your knee caps and could go on from there...

Does contentment become greater when pain has been greater? I find that idea perverse as well as incorrect. I do believe that the fear of future pain is greater if the actual horror of past pain is there, but I contend that this has nothing to do with the pleasure of contentment. Contentment is a positive entity. It doesn't need pain, disaster, unfairness, evil, or all those other things in order to be: it just is, and it would still be even if those supposed opposites did not exist at all. In fact, we know that contentment does still exist when some of the supposed opposites do not exist at all. Think of the eradication of polio. Do you feel less content because it is gone? I know I don't.

Now let's consider Heaven. Do we need Hell to make Heaven perfect, or can eternity with God stand on its own? (When you think about it, it does rather boggle the mind to think that we could even consider that God and Heaven might not have enough stuff on their own to make without the devil and Hell.)

Let's go back to our friends, the unborn. Let's say a fetus makes it to heaven and joins one of the many friendly chat groups up there. Do they all sit around whining about how they just can't appreciate heaven because they never were on earth to experience a bit of hell? Or are they really upset because they were never able to grasp the concept of Hell through good Sunday School tutelage? Or are they mad because no one else is in Hell? Get real. They aren't going to give a hoot about Hell; Hell isn't going to matter any more than hangnails will matter. Heaven is a positive entity, and it does not depend for its existence upon the presence of Hell.

Another thought: is the Hellion's need for Hell-so-we-can-have-a successful-Heaven based, not on literary snobbery, or on some esoteric balancing of opposites, but on the simple Hellion fact that if there were no Hell, the OTHERS, who should be in Hell while the Hellions are up in Heaven wouldn't be in Hell, but would be in Heaven with the Hellions? This would mean the good (officially saved) people would have been cheated! The possibility that this is the real motivation of the Hellions and the literary cognoscenti cannot be discounted. In fact, I think we need to keep it written on a flash card in red letters. It may just be the whole thing. We also need to remember the importance of Hell as part of the Company Line: there are plenty of people out there who are making their living—and a pretty good living it frequently is—out of Hell, whether they really believe in it or not.

Having trashed the need for Hell-as-an-opposite, let's get serious with our Sunday School time and think about grace and other things and their relation to Hell, salvation, Heaven, and life on earth.

Amazing Grace

For as long as I can remember, in scripture, in sermon, and in song, I have heard of God's amazing grace. Who doesn't love the old Irish slaver's hymn: "'Twas grace that made my heart to fear, and grace my fears relieved..." Grace seems to have worked for him, but under Hellion rules it doesn't seem to work for a lot of people (about 161 billion of them and counting, to be somewhat precise). However, under our new, recently adopted, Loving-God-whether-you-like-it-or-not rules, the Hellions and their rules are out and the God of Love is in charge. The God of Love, as it happens, has given us industrial strength grace that does work, and works every time for every soul. The Hellion idea that God was a wimp when it came to grace and that any one of us could tell God to go stuff it was troubling, so it is pleasing that God is being found to be able to cut the mustard when it comes to grace.

Grace seems to be the most wonderful thing that God could have supplied us with. Better than plastics, better than antibiotic drugs, better than the Grand Canyon, better than the Eiffel tower, better even than voice mail. Conventional wisdom to the contrary, like it or not, grace really is all-sufficient. Sadly, though, all-sufficient grace seems to be a problem for a good many people. For them it is hard to swallow the fact that we do not have to do anything to get the full eternal benefit of grace. We don't even have to accept it. Free Grace exists, in spite of the fact that lots of the people who tout grace very heavily seem, in the end, to believe that it really isn't God's gift, but that it is something that we can control by earning it, or at least by doing the "work" of accepting it. (Yes, the mere act of accepting is "work".)

In case anyone wants to introduce, and decry, "cheap grace", we must remember that grace is not cheap, it is free. There is an important difference. Grace can only be cheap if it has to be earned or paid for, and can be obtained with little sacrifice, but the actual situation is that we don't have to earn it. Whatever the cost may have been to God, She has made grace free to us. (Thank goodness, since we never could have earned it.) But what about the cost to God? Was there a cost to God? Would it cost you anything to forgive your children whom you love? Did God create us and give us the opportunity to do good and evil only to allow us to become such monsters that forgiving us is a particularly costly project for the very God who did it all? Or is God like any loving parent, wanting to forgive us…in fact long-ing to forgive us…and rushing to forgive us…and covering us with forgiving grace? Yes, that's the way God is and that is what God has done.

If the Alabama Baptists' survey is correct, and 46.1 percent of the people in Alabama, and a whole hellava lot of others, are going to Hell because grace didn't get them into heaven, I would have to think that Ol' Debil is scoring a lot of points in spite of God's professed love for each of us. And if that's true, it's a shame to see God get swatted around that way. Surely we aren't big enough to thwart God's efforts to give us grace, and surely the God who loves us isn't going to let the Ol' Debil get us—for eternity. Not if God can save us by grace. Hellions may think that God doesn't have the love (or the power) to save us in spite of ourselves, but they are wrong; He has saved us—ALL of us—for eternity.

There is a wonderful parallel between grace and gravity—just the sort of thing that would appeal to an engineer. Courtesy of The Ground of All Being, AKA the God of Love, gravity has always been here keeping us from flying off the face of the earth (in fact, it also keeps the face of the earth from flying off).

Nothing has been, or ever will be, created without reliance on gravity. Gravity pervades everything, and it makes our lives possible—whether we know it or not. So pervasive is gravity, that only the most perceptive of us would know it's here if Isaac Newton hadn't told us.

Newton's revelation about gravity did not usher gravity onto the earth, gravity was already here, working for people who had never heard of it. But Newton did bring gravity to our consciousness (not unlike Jesus bringing God's Love to our consciousness), and his revelation did make it possible for us to use gravity in ways that we couldn't when we didn't recognize it. Those who have heard of it and who have studied it can get more out of gravity than can those who are ignorant of it. But even those who are ignorant of the force of gravity benefit from it because they don't fly off the face of the earth any more than do those who are "washed" in gravity, and because of the engineers who design the superelevated curves that use gravity to keep cars on the road in a turn, and because of the engineers who design the bridges and structures so they can remain standing in spite of the stresses caused by gravity those who are "unwashed" in gravity still gain advanced benefit from it. All of these structures stand just as firmly for the people who have never heard of gravity, or who have heard and don't give a fig for it, as they stand for the true believers.

Grace gives all of us the same tender care we get from gravity, whether we believe in it or not, and whether we accept it or not. Love is eternal and is the elemental building block of the universe. God, the Creator and Ground of All Being, planned the universe with grace for all, and thanks to grace we are not doomed to go to hell by either our own hapless failures or our active, frantic efforts.

God sent Jesus to tell us about grace, not to create it. Scripture, in the first chapter of the Gospel of John, tells us that grace (The Word) was here from the beginning. Later, grace was with us in the person of Jesus, and grace still abounds. Grace was not merely a 32-year phenomenon; grace has been forever and it will be forever. Grace is here whether or not you hear about Jesus. Because of grace there is no place in Hell for you, or for me, or for anyone else.

All things considered (using engineering logic, of course), it seems clear that God really must be in charge of grace in spite of the idea some people have that they can control grace. If it's true that God is in charge of grace, and if God does want the best for us, and if Grace is all-sufficient, and if we can't stop it, alter it, or divert it, then why doesn't grace get us all into Heaven where God, according to scripture, wants us to end up? The answer, of course, is that grace does get all of us into heaven.

In spite of that assertion, an awful lot of people of the Christian faith, and other faiths as well, say that if you haven't believed the way they say you are supposed to have believed, the God who loves you is going to fry you for eternity, grace or no grace. (Saturday Night Live has certainly gotten a lot of miles out of that juxtaposition of incredible love and amazing hate, so why shouldn't we get some, too?) The Hellions' theory that gets us into this particular mess, is that God is a God of justice and righteousness as well as a God of love, and the love side of God loses out when it comes to salvation. Righteousness and justice take over and they are not user friendly. The Hellions don't go along with Job's gripe that God knows we can't get into heaven based on our goodness, and that we therefor don't have a chance for anything based on how good we are. The Hellions think that the fact that we aren't as good as God is just our tough luck, and if we can't make grace work, that is just some more of our tough luck.

So what about grace? Does it just park-in when justice and righteousness take over? "No! No!" say the justice and righteousness people, "Grace is always there for you, but you have to accept it." And if you don't accept it, your righteous God, in his wisdom, sends you to Hell—forever, even though He really loves you a whole lot more than you can even imagine. The fact is that Hellions really don't believe in grace: they believe in works that use grace. Here we go again; grace isn't sufficient after all; the work of accepting grace is what actually saves you. According to the Hellions, it's no matter that you never heard about grace in the first place: if you haven't accepted grace—it doesn't matter why—you are done for no matter what.

Well, thanks a lot God; I've known murderers (really, I have—I can think of two right now) who were more loving than that, and I just can't see why God, in His wisdom, can't be a whole, whole lot more loving than that. I want to see God succeed. I want love to win. I want grace to be sufficient for every one—regardless of race, creed, color, country of national origin, sexual preference, or whatever other divisive difference you can think of. I am remind of the religious operation in a nearby city that advertised itself as "A Place of Christian Worship for People of all Faiths". Strange as it seems, let's use that approach: let's go along with God and let everybody into Heaven, regardless of faith—or lack thereof.

What About The Final Judgment?

We need to spend some Sunday School time on the Final Judgment. Every body wants a final judgment, in fact a lot of folks are counting on it to burn a lot of other folks. It just wouldn't be fair not to have a final judgment. We have worked for our final judgment, we have sweated for our final judgment, and we deserve our final judgment. We have been expecting a final judgment since we were old enough to tie our own shoes, and, by God, we are going to have a final judgment or know why not.

Not to worry. You can relax, there is a final judgment: God does it and every body gets judged. Nobody skates by. Nobody gets special treatment. "Wait a minute", you might say, "I thought saved people were supposed to get special treatment! Why else would one get saved?" The realization that the saved aren't going to get special treatment may be a major disappointment, but it is still good news. Read on.

Most people who deal with the Final Judgment make the error of thinking in human time and thinking that the final judgment is final in human terms—something that happens at the end of human time on this earth. In fact, the Final Judgment is for all time, from the very beginning to the very end of everything. It is for eternity—based on God's timetable, not just for us using our timetable. God thought about the whole thing—you know God wouldn't handle a thing like eternity in Hell on a whim—and concluded that He couldn't wait until the end of human time to make the Final Judgment.

God did the job at the beginning, and went ahead right then and there and judged that every body was going to Heaven; She judged that there would be grace for everyone. She decided that GRACE WAS GOING TO WORK. Period. Whether YOU like it or not. God is not going to let you mess this up for yourself or anyone else. Eternity in Hell is just too big a thing to be left in your hands, in yo' mamma's hands, in the preacher's hands, in the hands of the Missionary Board, or in any other human hands.

We all mess up too frequently to be given a job as important as keeping the whole world out of Hell. (When you think about our record—and that includes our record at anything you might want to choose—it would be downright stupid for God to leave something as important as getting us into Heaven or Hell forever to screw-ups like us. Even at our best we have the potential to mangle almost anything at least part of the time, and that isn't good enough for an eternal judgment.)

God is in charge here, and He has decided that we all get to go to Heaven. All has been forgiven. That is the Final Judgment, and it has done been made. If you are a Presbyterian, you can consider this proof positive of predestination; if you are anything else, all you have to do is be thankful for it.

There isn't any Hell—except the Hell we create here on earth for our own personal use. The only thing out there is Heaven. Everybody goes, and everybody loves it when they get there. For a lot of people, this may be hard to take. For as long as you can remember, you have been counting on the warm feeling of having all those other people in Hell—and all of a sudden they are going to Heaven. What a let down! They don't deserve it because they haven't been nearly as good as you have. But then, of course, when you think about it, you haven't been that good yourself, so you really don't deserve heaven either. (If you think you have been good enough to deserve Heaven, go directly to Hell, do not pass Go, do not collect $200.)

How about virtue? If getting into Heaven depended upon our virtue, we would be in trouble no matter what, so thank goodness for grace. Like the rain, it falls on the good and the evil alike. So, as good as you are, you still need grace—maybe a lot of it—and as bad as they, the worse-than-you, are, grace is still sufficient for them. There is still evil, and some folks out there are evil beyond imagination. We haven't been able to get evil behind us so far, and that means part of our job in Sunday School is to study on how we can stay as far away from evil as possible. Most of the time, when it comes to a really tough decision involving good and evil, we are like the Congress and the Legislature, and just mill around trying to figure out which way is up. Hopefully Sunday School will help God deliver us from evil. (I seem to remember something about that in the Lord's Prayer.)

Remember: God went ahead and made the final judgment—for all time—right at the beginning. God has handed down the judgment that every body goes to Heaven, so don't you try to get in the way—just go quietly when your time comes. The judgment has been made and God is well pleased with it (Genesis 1:31).

What About the Fall?

The Fall is another good Sunday School topic. People notice that there seems to be a certain level of disconnect between us and God, and lots of folks have made an ongoing big deal about trying to explain that situation. The buzz word is that we are "broken", and the explanation is that there was "a Fall" (The Fall) and that we were the ones who fell. By using the term "fall" we have trapped ourselves into explaining Adam and Eve's thing as a precipitous descent from something good to something bad. Because Eve gave Adam the apple, some men who are into blaming, blame her—and women in general—for the whole thing. The women who don't try to worm their way out of blame for the fall claim that it just shows that women are so smart they have been leading men around by their noses from the beginning; others do try to worm their way out of the blame. People who are big enough say it was really nobody's fault: just one of those things. Of course, it is a "thing" that is being blamed for sending to Hell everybody who hasn't been lucky enough to be "redeemed". Some thing.

But, let's look at it this way: It was the fruit of the tree of the knowledge of good and evil that the young couple ate, and it has been said that by doing so they attempted to be like God, and thus fell from a friendly relationship with God and from God's grace—that is to say, they got on God's bad list. NOTE: If you are a God-of-Power person and try to blame this situation on Adam and Eve, you might find yourself backed into the corner of having to admit—or at least slither yourself away from—the idea that if God really was in charge, HE is the one who made them eat the apple, so there really wasn't a fall: it was just another case of following orders from above—like all of Hitler's concentration camp guards.

There is another way to look at the situation resulting from the said action and the action itself. Let us consider that rather than falling from God, the young couple rose toward God and thereby entered an estate much more demanding than the one they had inhabited in Eden, and one that, for the first time, was human. God was in charge and the event involving the humans and the tree was when God made Her gift of life to us. Before the said action, humans didn't have a moral life, they just existed like the other animals.

Before the fateful bite, Adam and Eve must have been just like the other animals of the garden: they were totally innocent of good and evil, and were operating on the basis of instinct alone. Apparently they knew nothing of God except that God was The Man and that it was good fun to have a chat with God at the end of a long day of plucking food off of low hanging branches. If you have had your own Dachshund, or perhaps your own lion, it is easy to see all of this. It is possible that the said Dachshund opens his little eyes and sees God first thing every morning, and again after every nap of the day. He may well have a daily chat with God. I can see both of them enjoying it. But, the dog has no inkling of the difference between good and evil. He just does what instinct tells him to do, and gives not a thought for whether it might be good or evil, or even a thought for whether there might be such things as good and evil.

The dog can be most affectionate—loving, we might say— and he can make himself appear to be good by learning what not to do. Not that that he deals with things in any moral sense, it's just that he can fairly easily figure out that it is better to not get swatted on his nose than to get swatted for peeing on the rug. Hence, no soiled rugs. Hence, he looks good. Hence, also, no moral judgment, just a desire to avoid getting swatted. I'll bet good money that Adam and Eve potty trained very quickly too— and with no moral content to the act. And they probably had just as much fun as the Dachshunds and the lions, too—just doing what comes naturally and having nice chats with God from time to time. Nothing in the Bible suggests otherwise.

So what happened? Was the fruit of the tree of the knowledge of good and evil the poison that separated woman and man from God because of their (apparently innocent) hubris? No. Did it doom them to Hell? No. Was it the biggest screw-up of all time? No.

If it wasn't the ticket to damnation, then what was the fruit of the tree of good and evil? It was a revelation. (There is another one of them at the other end of the Bible.) Eating the fruit opened Adam's and Eve's eyes. The fact that they realized they diddn' have no pants on, although highly reported, was really a nothing item. The big item was that, for the first time, they realized there was a moral dimension to life. The knowledge of good and evil raised them above the Dachshunds and fox terriers and put them into the moral heavy lifting business. Once they knew about good and evil, there was no backing away from morality. As the lawyers say "once rung, the bell cannot be unrung." The knowledge of good and evil made them human. It made them realize that life had its share of hell. It made life more interesting than mere existence, and it gave life a purpose beyond just eating and chatting with God.

For the first time, they could be good and they could do good. They could get beyond their own needs and worry about the needs of others. They could have the satisfaction of a job done well, and the shame of a poor performance, because they knew the difference. In spite of what might appear to have been a good start, while Adam and Eve did get a glimmer of the fact that God is love, they did not become fully Godlike. All we have to do to prove their lack of success is to look around at Adam and Eve's children—us—and see by our actions how far from God we are. Even though they did not make it to God-in-training status, or anything close to it, Adam and Eve did have revealed to them how tough and how wonderful it might be even to try to be like God.

So there was no fall, there was a revelation—I suppose this was the very first one. This would mean there was no fall from which we need to be redeemed. God gave the young couple a magnificent opportunity: they were given the chance to be children of God, and spend their lives trying to live up to that status. The game was afoot, and we have been playing it ever since. [Note to alert reader: It is at about this point that the theologically trained expert mutters something about ignoring the "salvific work of Jesus" and the hellion lurches into a diatribe about "being washed in the blood of the lamb." Both are

referred to the section of this volume titled *BigJesus LittleJesus.*
Yes, we are a mess and messes do have to be cleaned up, but God
realized that before the beginning and took care of it. We aren't
fallen, but, then, we do stay lost almost all of the time.]

Oh, And One More Thing…

If the preceding hasn't provided a lot of fun in Sunday School
and hasn't convinced you that Hell has been vanquished, then
probably nothing else will. Nevertheless, in spite of the low odds
of it making any difference, here is an additional thought:

For most of us life here on earth is pretty good, even border-
ing on the ecstatic at times, but life isn't that good all the time.
Husbands, wives, and children die much too young, and for no
good reason (God really didn't need, or want, to use that auto
crash to take little Johnny, in spite of what a lot of well-meaning
people will say). People make dumb mistakes or get drunk one
time too many and snuff out multiple lives in grinding automobile crashes. Terrorists strike and kill, one death at a time, or ten,
or a hundred, or thousands. Lives are ground to dust by horrible
illness that take forever before the blessing of death finally arrives.
Pol Pot and company murder virtually an entire civilization
and enchain everyone who is left alive. "Our holocaust" leaves a
mark of terror and evil on the world, and is only the latest in an
apparently never-ending line of holocausts. The history of the
world chronicles one plunder, rape, slaughter, battle, and war after
another. The same people and their grandkids do it to each other
time after time for hundreds of years. Ethnic hate never gives in,
yet it never conquers all—it just keeps on trying. Genocide is
nothing new and nothing suggests that genocide is going away.
Problem after problem piles on to people who begin with only

a modest chance for a decent life, and that chance gets crushed. Drugs smash lives. Insanity robs life of its reason for being. Rulers who could release people from bondage instead forge stronger and stronger chains. Nature gives us tornadoes, cyclones, tidal waves, volcanic eruptions, avalanches, hurricanes, floods, forest fires, earthquakes, droughts, searing heat, and unbearable cold. The forgotten die alone, and the good die young.

Remember, we have AIDS, Alzheimer's, Lou Gherig's disease, Down's Syndrome, schizophrenia, bi-polar disorder, cancer of the almost everything, Eisenmenger's Syndrome, primary pulmonary hypertension, epilepsy, spina bifida, cholera, polio (but maybe not for much longer unless certain government leaders continue to make sure polio can flourish in their countries), small pox, juvenile onset diabetes, anthrax, dyptheria, incest, statutory rape, date rape, aggravated rape, regular ol' rape, West Nile fever, viral hemorrhagic fever (Ebola virus), tularemia, botulism, plague, Ricin, mustard gas, Sarin, black lung, whooping cough, scarlet fever, infectious mononucleosis, eczema, hives, cholera, chorea, croup, dysentery, Erysipelas, Leprosy, Osteomyelitis, rheumatic fever, scrofula, trench mouth, tuberculosis, tularemia, undulant fever, frostbite, gangrene, radiation sickness, histoplasmosis, Lumpy Jaw, scurvy, Pellagra, rickets, beriberi, Rocky Mountain Spotted Fever, Cystic Fibrosis, blindness, deafness, elephantiasis, hookworm, Lala-Azar, malaria, roundworm, tapeworm, mumps, the common cold, Dengue Fever, Encephalitis, Hepatitis, herpes of various kinds, measles, Mosaic Disease (your guess is as good as mine), rabies, shingles, pneumonia, Yellow Fever, foot and mouth disease, mad cow disease, manslaughter, murder 2, mass murder, regular ol' murder, torture, child abuse, sexual child abuse, spousal abuse, elder abuse, regular ol' abuse, burglary, robbery, assault, assault and battery, assault with the intent to commit murder, drive-by shooting, destruction of life and ending of life by drug abuse, harassment, stalking, stupid generals sending tens of thousands of men to their deaths, smart generals sending tens of thousands of men to their deaths, Final Solutions, ethnic cleansing, turf wars, bullying, ethnic hate, race hate, class hatred, historic hatred, regular ol' hate, extortion, fraud, simony (not much, but we still do it!), greed, gluttony, lust, laziness, carelessness, flood, forest fire, earthquake, hurricane, typhoon, tornado, drought, famine, blizzard, freezing to death, shark attack, poisonous snake bite, being torn apart by wild animals, wage slavery, regular ol' slavery, indifference, injustice of so many kinds they can't be named, treason, terrorism, shipwreck, boiler explosion, bad uglies, plane crash, railroad wreck, structural failure caused by ignorance, structural failure caused by carelessness, design flaws in automobiles, elevators, aircraft, space craft, ships, and anything else designed and made by humans, careless mistakes, willful negligence, hubris, megalomania, blindness, deafness, bizarre mental problems like thinking you are your own hat, etc., bizarre physical problems like having no immune system, etc., sudden infant death syndrome, Munchausenism by proxy, Sadism, pederasty, bestiality, kleptomania, larceny after trust, embezzlement, land mines, unexploded artillery shells, exploded artillery shells, poison gasses, electrocution (accidental and otherwise), drowning, slipping and falling from high places, trench cave-ins, being crushed by backhoes, being killed, injured, disabled, or brain damaged by things that break due to metallurgical flaws, scalding to death when the main steam pipe breaks, dying of thirst in the desert or in the ocean, getting dragged into a Mafia fight and winding up dead by mistake, failure, KKK attack, "religious" leaders who lead their flocks to death or terrorism, "faith healers" who don't have faith in anything beyond the dollar and who don't heal, people who do a sorry job, laziness, avarice, flatterers, sociopaths, psychopaths, lust, pride, envy, anger, gluttony, and a number of other hellish things. We have quite enough Hell on earth.

Try as we might, there are times, too many of them, when we just don't know what is right. What we would not do, we do, and what we would do, we do not. There's no need for God to lay any more of that hell on us, as God surely knows. So, because we have plenty of hell on earth, including a lot of types that we have not mentioned, there isn't going to be any Hell beyond earth. We are left with everyone going to Heaven—the good, the not so good, and the bad alike. Hope this isn't a disappointment.

Oh Well, One More Thing—The Hitler Thing

When you start talking about everyone going to Heaven, some whiner invariably brings up the question of whether A. Hitler is there. How could he be? After all, he unleashed a war that claimed over twenty million lives. How could a killer of that magnitude make it to Heaven—the same Heaven where good people like us aspire to be?

It is a tough question, particularly when you consider it from the human point of view, so let's take a Sunday School hour to deal with Herr Schickelgrubber. I can't forgive Hitler. You can't forgive Hitler. Nobody in his or her right mind can forgive or forget Hitler. We would all simply erase his existence from the face of the earth if we could, and expect that whoever replaced him would at least be better, and hopefully a whole lot better.

So how does Hitler qualify for Heaven, or Ghengis Khan, or the terrorist called Xxxx, or all the other super-murderers? The answer, of course, is that they don't qualify. They get in on grace.

They get in because of love divine, which excels all loves, particularly any love we humans can come up with. And they wouldn't get in without that divine love, because we sure wouldn't let them in. But there they are.

A couple of thoughts come to mind. First: we are agreed that these people are horrendous mutations, but we have to look for that line in the sand. Just exactly when did they go from being just bad to being horrendous mutations? There had to be that one sin that pushed them across the line, and we have already talked about how unfair it would be to send that fellow in the remote village to Hell forever because of that one sin too many. I don't see any way around having to use the same logic for mass murderers.

You might say, "Oh, no, no, no! Hitler and the rest of that crowd left the line way far behind them and would qualify for Hell regardless of where the line was back there in their dust." Perhaps that's true, depending upon where the line really is drawn, but what about the small-time mass murderer who just does one too many? Is the second murder the charm? Or does it take more? Somebody is going to Hell forever for just one sin too many, and that turns the whole system into an uncomfortable mess.

Then you have to factor in the environment. Was Hitler's mother or father—or both of them—a sick character who damaged poor little Hitler beyond repair? Was he abused as a child? Did his experiences as a lowly soldier in World War I scar him beyond what a weak psyche could take? What about the political-economic system into which he came of age? What about all the other crazy, or crazed, people who carried out his orders, almost without being asked in many cases? What about the fact that if all the stars hadn't fallen into place he would never have become Chancellor of the Third Reich and, not having all the resources of the German people at his fingertips, might never have become anything but a particularly obnoxious civil servant—say an old-style postal clerk? Hitler didn't do it all himself. In fact, there is no evidence that Hitler, himself, ever killed even one single person.

Next you have to think about Hitler and the Mark Twain effect. We don't know all that happened during those final hours in Hitler's bunker under the rubble of Berlin. What if Hitler finally saw the error of his ways, and his last words to his beloved Eva Braun were, "Eva, I have seen the error of my ways. My evil has been of unimaginable proportions, but I have found Jesus and I die secure in the promise of life eternal, made sure in the death and resurrection of God's son, Jesus Christ our Lord. Amen. Farewell, cruel world. Farewell, Eva." BANG! Of course Eva can't tell us whether or not it happened that way since she died, too. Maybe she found Jesus, too.

Suppose Hitler's story actually did end in such a way. How would you feel about meeting Hitler in Heaven if he had had that ten seconds of salvation before he pulled the trigger? Would you walk right up and shake hands with him and tell him how glad you were to meet him? Somehow, I don't see it. You and me and Hitler are all lucky that he got in on grace, and not on that irritating thirty second salvation special.

Amazingly, we can see that even with Hitler there are mitigating circumstances, and we have to remember that we are talking about eternal punishment. More important, we are also talking about the love of God, all loves excelling. Forget human love, it isn't in play. Forget human vengeance, it isn't in play. In fact, vengeance is not in play at all: the scriptures tell us that God said "vengeance is mine". People tend to think that, having taken vengeance for His own, God was planning to use it. They forget that God is love, and have a hard time accepting the (radically new?) idea that having taken vengeance for Her own, God simply isn't going to use it, She has sequestered vengeance forever. Now that vengeance is out of the picture, we can forget justice as well—that is, you can forget human justice or our human idea of what God's justice might be like—justice is not in play either—at least not when it comes to deciding who goes to heaven.

Remember, God is love. We don't fully understand God (we are still looking through the glass darkly), and that has to mean that God's love is beyond our understanding. Seen darkly or not, we have scriptural reasons to believe that God's love is better, more effective, more efficient, and more downright unbelievably wonderful than anything we can come up with and that God errs on the side of being more loving rather than less loving. Sounds like grace.

So how is Heaven going to work? In accordance with scripture, of course. "We will not all die, but we will all be changed..." (I Cor. 15: 51). We will have to wait to find out what we are going to be changed into, but it appears to me that it will be something—and somebody—who will neither recognize Hitler or be recognized as Hitler. Hitler is a special case, but there are lots of other similar, smaller caliber cases. If your mother were a drunken shrew who made your life on earth a misery, would you want to meet the old bat in Heaven? Not likely, but wouldn't it be nice to meet the heavenly mother whom you never had on earth? Want to meet the guy who raped you, got you pregnant and gave you AIDS? Didn't think so. But how about meeting the heavenly person he has become by the Grace of God? (Remember, thank God, he will have been transformed—and so will you.)

It would be easy to go on and on with this, but the bottom line—even without Hitler and his ilk—is that we need that transformation en route to Heaven. All of us need transformation, even you and I. Admit it, we know we aren't perfect. We remember an endless list of things we wish we hadn't done or said to someone, and we aren't looking forward to having our victims recognize us in Heaven, are we? So it's love, grace, transformation, and the greatest of these is that we get all three.

RESEARCH FINDINGS: THIRD HALF

In the Second Half, using impeccable logic, bold leaps of faith, and commendable persistence, we did a number on Hell. It is, as we say "toast". As a result, the nether world has pretty much become history, and we have had to grapple with the question of what value religion might have in a system in which no one gets fried.

We recognize that some people simply are not going to be happy with a God who doesn't send anyone to Hell, but, as much as we regret it, we are going to have to leave those folks behind. Fortunately for them God still loves them whether we leave them behind or not. Those "left behind" are happy—they all know that after The Rapture we will all be driving their cars through Hell. Those of us who don't feel it can hardly imagine the comfort of that feeling, but for those who do, it beats being a hog in slop. It's nice that no matter how we view God's love, we can all be happy about the fact that we are going to end up in Heaven in spite of ourselves—and whether or not we think anyone else will be up there with us.

Happily for the operators of Sunday Schools, we have

concluded that, given our state of continuing depravity—as exemplified by the problems of moral entropy and the US Congress, we each have a lifetime job trying to figure out first, how to keep out of trouble, and second, how to rise above zero and actually do some good while we are here living the days that The Lord has given us. We have bumbled into the realization that the old approach to Sunday School is not going to work—instead, we are going to have to embrace a new paradigm.

The New Paradigm

Please note that the following, which suggests a significant change in how we view religion, is not mere drive-by iconoclasm. It is large caliber iconoclasm, carefully considered, and worth a good argument, if you want to have one. Sunday School would be a nice place to do the arguing. Without Hell to spur us on, and facing Heaven no matter what we do because God really does love us with a love that is unconditional, we have to think about—and practice—religion in a way that will be new for many of us. No longer will we be able to hang our religion on the Fire Insurance peg. When it comes to religion, we are going to have to find and accept a new paradigm.

The elements of the new paradigm are something along these lines:

- God is love. That would seem to mean that love is God, and that as we apply love in our lives we approach God—or that we cannot approach God without love.
- Hell is gone, so our notions of how to live with hell need to go with hell because they do not apply to life with a loving God.

- No longer will religious life be measured by what we believe.
- No longer will religious life be measured by whom we know (Jesus, or Muhammad, for instance).
- No longer will religious life by measured by how many times—leaning toward a minimum of two—that we have been born.
- No longer will religious life be measured by whether or not God talks to us.
- No longer will religious life be measured by our membership in a church.
- No longer will religious life be measured by whether we are one of the washed-in-the-blood-of-the-lamb, or one of the unwashed.

Our religion is going to boil down to what we do. Love and compassion are going to be the big things.

Thankfully, we can be comforted by the knowledge that our religion and the religious life that flows from it have nothing to do with whether or not we end up in Heaven or Hell—which is lucky, given who and what we are. Our religious life is the reflection of whether or not we believe that we really are children of God and want to live like children of God. We are going to have to face—and hopefully rejoice in—the fact that the things we do will be the important stuff of our religion. We are going to have to face the fact that what we say we believe will be used not to get us into Heaven, but to set the benchmark for how much we fail to live up to our faith—because fail we will. We will not lose sight of the fact that we are like Paul in that, "that which we would, we do not, and that which we would not, we do".

The things we do will be the only palpable evidence of whether we know Jesus, or Buddha, or Allah, or any other god or person. If we have been born more than once, our second birth will have nothing to do with whether or not we end up in Heaven or Hell; the real fruit of our second birth will be what it has done to help us live as children of the God of Love today, right where we are. If God talks to us, how well we do and how loving our actions are will be the only proof of what God might have said—and telling people that God told you to do it is no longer going to be a successful excuse for a major screwup.

We aren't going to be judged by God based on what we do, as we might have thought would happen under the old paradigm. Instead, under the new paradigm everyone who sees what we do, hears what we say, or benefits from or suffers because of what we do, will judge us for who we are. If we claim to have been told what to do by God, the people we interact with are going to judge God based on our actions. We will need to be careful not to give God a bad name, because in the end we won't be able to blame what we do on God—or the devil. We are going to have to realize that whether or not we stand up in front of humankind to be counted, humankind is going to count us. What we do will be ours—we will no longer be able to blame it on God. In short, we are going to have to live up to our bumper stickers. For those who live under the new paradigm, it isn't going to be easy to be someone who will be proud of the way he or she has represented God: grace isn't cheap—it's free—but there is still a cross to bear.

Everyone down here can measure us, and a lot of them will, but fortunately for us, God is not going to be measuring how far we have carried the Cross. God isn't going to be measuring anything, She is just gonna' keep on spreading grace.

INTERLUDE

Let me stop just a moment and say a few kind words about the good Baptists of Alabama, whose survey statistics have been figuring so prominently in this discussion. The truth is that they show up so often simply because they are the ones from whom we have the figures. As far as I know, the Baptists of Alabama—and perhaps a few other Baptists here and there—are the only people in the entire United States who have had the concern and have gone to the effort to figure out how many souls they have yet to save. They are doing their best for all of us.

The folks in Alabama have just as good a chance to get to heaven as the folks anywhere else have, and they may actually be way ahead of the people in your neighborhood. So, when Alabama gets cited you have to remember that the 53.1% saved statistic is probably equivalent to the best chance anyone anywhere has of getting to Heaven (based on Hellion theology, that is). And, of course, lots of people, not having heard the Gospel, or having heard it from some shrew who irritated the tar out of them instead of saving them, just don't have any chance at all by Hellion-measure.

The Baptists' hearts are in the right place, even if their heads don't seem to be.

End Of Interlude

END OF BOOK

W e have covered a lot of important ground, crushed many a long-revered doctrine, made our own brand of history, and have had some good fun doing it. We have squashed Hell flat as a flounder. That is not a bad day's work, and on top of getting rid of Hell we have landed in the middle of the new religious paradigm. In spite of all of these laudable accomplishments, I am left wondering about a few things:

- What will the Major Motion Picture of this book be like?
- Who will play the author? Robert DeNiro, William H. Macy, Homer Simpson?
- Where do we go from here? Maybe we should go to Sunday School and work on how to live the rest of our lives. We can also devote ourselves to getting rid of hell. Why not?

The End

APPENDIX

Hellion Rules for Going To Hell

1. The sinner qualifies for his or her level of eternal torment in hell by performance. Merely thinking about the offense does not count in the eternal sense. Thinking about it can, however, get you into trouble on an earthly level because you can torment your self and even provoke other types of offenses by simply thinking about the subject offense. If you are rash enough to allow thought to become the mother of action, you can get into trouble for eternity, so be careful about thinking, particularly if you are trying to chew gum at the same time.

2. Efficiency counts. Thus, if you are particularly successful at your chosen offense you will be lowered at least one level based on your degree of efficiency, and dazzlingly successful sinners can be lowered two levels. (This is very rare and calls forth considerable admiration from even the most hardened Hell-watchers. There is a Wall of Dishonor.)

3. The definitions below are binding in any court of record, and a finding that you have been guilty of said same offense will cause you to go to Hell forever. If you are cunning enough to sneak past the lower courts, Saint Peter will get you at the Pearly Gates, so there is no use trying to fake it. It won't impress anyone but your friends, and you know what trash they are.

4. The definitions below are hereby Certified Correct.

5. You always go to the level dictated by your worst offense. Lesser-included offenses do not add to your score, however lesser offenses that are not included do.

6. All judgments as to what is major and what is minor are also hereby Certified Correct.

7. If you think your case needs adjudication, just e-mail. We have a special court in Level 2 that takes care of that. We'll get you on the docket just as soon as those ahead of you have been taken care of.

8. If you have any gripes about any of this, please see No.7, above.

9. Qualification for merit award:

Merit Award category (This isn't actual Hell, so it's not too bad, really):

- 0-1 You just can't believe they really did that...
- 0-2 You can't believe they even thought about it
- 0-3 How in Hell could anybody have done that more than once?
- 0-4 Repeatedly carrying out an act that, with bad luck, could cause actual damage (if you cause the damage you will qualify for Hell)
- 0-5 Too dumb for words (There are no laws against

being stupid, so it is only fitting that those who work at it be given some form of recognition.)

Notes to Rules

1. Up is toward heaven and Level 1. Down is toward Level 4.
2. No adjustment upward is possible from Level 4.
3. Eligibility based on four or more violations automatically qualifies the winner for immediate and permanent transfer one level further down. This is known as a "Stuff", and the Stuff moves the winner down one level from the lowest level mentioned in the scoring—no matter where the Stuff may appear in the scoring list.
4. The inability of a politician to frame in his (or her) own mind a sentence with a subordinate clause and then say it with his own mouth immediately places the politician on NOAA's "Hell Watch" status. ("Hell Warning" is worse. You are usually in actual descent before the word that you are in Warning status has reached you.)
5. Winning the Nobel Peace Prize will raise you one level (except see Note 2).
6. In case of disputes or confusion about which level the candidate qualifies for due to multiple qualifications, the All-Dominant Hell Operating Committee (also called ADHOC committee) will make the call. (The Evil One himself—no not Saddam—regularly calls on this group for advice.)
7. There are a few secret qualifications and rules that we are unable to reveal in a family book on Hell. Be assured that they are all necessary and proper. Also be assured that if you qualify under one of those rules, you will be

personally notified and the rule will be explained to your full satisfaction. In fact, you may learn more about it than you really wanted to know.

8. Remember that being a leader makes it a lot easier for you to go to Hell (and to Heaven, as well, but that's another story).

9. Corporate, institutional, and team clients go to Hell immediately upon qualifying, unlike other clients who only arrive after death. Strangely, corporate, etc., get to leave Hell upon death and can qualify to leave at any time if they turn over a new leaf. THESE THINGS ARE NOT TRUE FOR INDIVIDUAL APPLICANTS.

10. Excuses that don't work (Fair warning: just don't bother with these. We are real, real tired of them and sometimes due to infraction of rules 1-3, 2-2, 2-6, or 3-8, you may find yourself on the bottom end of a Stuff that will actually demote you a level for your trouble.):

   1) *"I didn't know the gun was loaded."*
   2) *"I just had a couple of drinks, officer..."*
   3) *"Hitler did it first!"*
   4) *"It wasn't as bad as what Osama did!"*
   5) *"It wasn't as bad as what Saddam did!"*
   6) *"But, but, Eve told me to do it!"*
   7) *"I was under orders."*
   8) *"I forgot."*
   9) *"It was Bill Clinton's fault."*
   10) *"It was Hillary Clinton's fault."*
   11) *"It was _____'s fault."*

11. Excuses that might work:

   1) *"I was trying my best, but..."* (Note that this can be dangerous: if you really weren't trying your best, you

could get a Stuff.)
2) *Being stupid might work, but if you are smart enough
   to try this one, you are too smart for it to work.*

Just so we can be sure we are all together on the rules, let's do
a test case. Hey, why not use a right-wing type radio talk show
host as our example?!!

Given the drivel that he puts out personally and the mindless
drivel he sucks (that giant sucking sound again) out of his callers,
your average talk show host would definitely qualify under 1-2,
2-1, 2-3, 2-4, 3-5, 3-6, 4-1, and 4-3. With any kind of typical
megalomania, he would probably qualify as well under 2-5, 3-8,
4-2, 4-4, 4-5, and 4-6. Since 8 is more than 4 and 14 is even
more more than 4, our test victim would qualify under note 3 for
level 4 with 3 downward level transfers. (The in-group calls these
downward transfers "Stuffs", because they found themselves so
frequently singing out in a happy chorus, "Stuff him down one
more level!") Keep in mind, of course, that you can't actually go
below Level 4, but if you are down there with extra Stuffs, you
get to go to one of the Special Rooms. The only good thing about
being in a Special Room is that you can have your hairdresser
flown in from L.A. to do your hair once a week.

The ADHOC committee calls the above score a 4 (3), [Level
Four with 3 stuffs] and can tell you that you are going to meet
some really interesting people down there—some about whom
you have read in your history books and newspapers, and others
who will be real surprises. Enjoy!

Now and then these rules and notes are cited by number in
the text just to make a point—for your edification, of course.
When there is no citation, you can amuse your self as you read
by deciding which rule the various denizens of Hell who are

mentioned hereafter qualified under, or by noting additional rules under which they could (and do) qualify. Keep a little score card; it will be fun. Actually, this could become a great parlor game. All rights are hereby reserved. (You can try this on your friends, fellow Xxxxxxxxxx National Committee Members, Sunday School teachers, etc.)

One of the beautiful things about figuring out who is going to Hell is that you can do your research anytime, anywhere. You can do useful research in church, in parking lots, on the highway, at the Rotary Club, at your house, on the high seas, in the air (surrounded by an airplane, of course), at the cinema, at highly-cultural cultural events, at parties, in ditches, at school, at work, while viewing TV, while listening to the radio, while reading, from California to the New York island, in Patagonia, in Berkeley Square, on the Grand Canal, on the Nile, and on and on. It is so effortless; it is so fulfilling; it is so rewarding; it is just plain beautiful. It's like being an airline pilot; you can't believe someone will actually pay you to do something you love so much.

You have your own favorite places for research on Hell— whether you have thought of them that way or not. Now, of course, you can think of them that way. Let your mind drift back to the last time you crossed paths with someone who definitely needed to go to Hell. Evaluate the candidates carefully, and make an assignment; don't hesitate to give 'em what they really deserve, after all Hell is only for ever.

Printed in the United States
96568LV00002B/108/A